Forty Days of Meditations

Lydia M. Douglas

Published by Prioritybooks Publications

Florissant, Missouri

P. O. Box 2535
Florissant, Mo 63033

Copyright ©2016 by
Lydia M. Douglas

All Rights reserved. No part of this book may be reproduced or transmitted in any forms by any means, electronic, mechanical, photocopy, recording or otherwise, without the consent of the Publisher, except as provided by USA copyright law.

All scriptures are taken from the King James Version of the Holy Bible.

This book is a work of nonfiction. The incidents, characters, and dialogue are products of the author's experiences.

Edited by: Kendra Koger & Lamia Ashley

Cover Designed by Sheldon Mitchell of Majaluk

Manufactured in the United States of America

Library of Congress Control Number: 2016955991

ISBN: 978-0989650267

For information regarding discounts for bulk purchases, please contact Prioritybooks Publications at 1-314-306-2972 or rosbeav03@yahoo.com.

To contact the author, please email her at: ldoug48305@aol.com. You can also visit her at www.booksbylydia.com.

Forty Days of Meditations

Lydia M. Douglas

Dedication

This book is dedicated to everyone that needs the help of God. He promised us He would give us joy and peace. All we have to do is keep our mind stayed on Him. No matter what He allows us to go through, He is our keeper during both day and night. Meditation strengthens our personal relation with God.

This book is dedicated to my late husband and to my three sons, Gerry Sr., Mark Sr., and James, Jr., who are very supportive and have helped me deal with my loss in the passing of my husband, James.

I want to thank all of the readers that supports my work. Thank you for the speaking engagements, the calls, and letters of support. I appreciate you all!

God is truly our resource and our help in times of need. I give Him all the glory.

Day 1

"Every New Morning My Victory is On the Way"

Psalms 34:17-22

"The righteous cry out, and the Lord hears, and delivers them out of all their troubles. The Lord is near to those who have a broken heart, And saves such as have a contrite spirit. Many are the afflictions of the righteous, But the Lord delivers him out of them all. He guards all his bones; not one of them is broken. Evil shall slay the wicked, And those who hate the righteous shall be condemned. The Lord redeems the soul of His servants, And none of those who trust in Him shall be condemned."

We all go through seasons of difficulties and challenges in life. One of Satan's traps is to isolate us and convince us that we will not make it through. He pushes us to lack faith and to stay away from those who want us to live healthy lives.

But we serve a God that has compassion for us and it is renewed every morning; His love for us is renewed every day. When He allows us to see another day, that is His love, His grace and mercy which never fails. No matter what He allows us to go through, victory is on the way.

Satan has no power because Victory belongs to God. All we have to do is stay connected to our Lord and Savior Jesus Christ. We are blessed because with each new day He is giving us another chance to make today better than yesterday.

However, this isn't to ignore the fact that we are going to face negativity and tribulations through our daily walks. In 1 Corinthians 15:31 Paul says, "I die daily" but that was in relation to Romans 8:36: "For Your sake we are killed all day long; We are accounted as sheep for the slaughter."

There is a price to pay on this earth for following Christ, and there are those who are going to try to persecute us. But, within all that, we have the promise of protection in a Holy realm. With that, there is a new beginning each and every day. All we have to do is praise Him and give Him thanks for what He has done and is going to do in our lives.

We know the victory is already won, we just have to wait on God, and His time is not our time. Psalms 34:19 tells us: "Many are the afflictions of the righteous, but the Lord delivers him out of them all." That verse is proof that Satan has no victory over our lives.

We are called Righteous because of our relationship with Jesus Christ, the one that shed His Blood and died on the cross for us. When we stay connected to Christ, all we have to do is keep the faith in Him and His Word will come to pass.

There are two verses that teach that God is for us. They are Psalms 34:9: "Oh fear the Lord, you His saints! There is no want to those who fear Him." And Psalms 34:10 tells us: "The young lions lack and suffer hunger; But those that seek the Lord shall not lack any good thing."

He already knows the trials, tribulations, struggles and hard times we will face. But He is there for them all. Our Victory is on the way. He said He would delivery us out of them all, and His Word is true and it will come to pass.

We will lack nothing.

As lamented in the popular song by Kirk Franklin, He will "never put more on me than I can bear." That lets us know that He will be with us in the midst of our storms. We can and will get through all of them. He did not tell us the road would be easy, but through His Word, He promised that He would never leave us, nor forsake us.

We become strong from his promises and that is where we draw our strength. He also said, "The Joy of the Lord is your strength," (Nehemiah 8:10b) so all we have to do is stand because our Victory is on the way. While we are on the way to victory, we can and should give Him praise, because that is where our strength comes from.

As long as we have faith and patience, we will inherit all of the promises He has made for us.

So we can thank God for Victory in the name of Jesus.

Questions

What kinds of struggles or difficulties do you feel you are dealing with today?

_____
_____
_____
_____

Is having faith in God easy for you? Why?

_____
_____
_____
_____

Do you have everything you need? What are you missing and why?

_____
_____
_____
_____

Do you believe in God's promises? Why or why not?

_____
_____
_____
_____

Day 2

"With Christ on my Side, Nothing Can Stop Me."

Philippians 4:13

"I can do all things through Christ who strengthens me."

Life can be rough sometimes. God did not tell us the road would be easy, and with all of the negativity that is broadcasted daily, boy, do we know it.

Sometimes we might feel as if we are coming up on the rough side of the mountain. Through those bumpy times, where the dust is flying in our eyes, and our vision is impaired, The Word tells us to hold on, our victory is on the way.

The rough side of the mountain has places where we can hold on to and move one step at a time. If it was smooth, we would slide all the way down. So let's not complain about the rough side; it will help us get to the top of our destination where God wants us to be.

Just as our text reminded us in Philippians 4:13: "I can do all things through Christ who strengthens me." Remember this when you are going through some harsh times, if we do it God's way, we will come out victorious.

We have another reminder in Romans 8:37: "…in all of these things we are more than conquerors through Him who loved us."

If we live our lives God's way, we will come out of all of the problems we are facing and will face.

The reason we can live through all of the trauma we face, is because we do not own our own ability to fix the situations, but just as Paul said, he can do all things through Christ who strengthens him. As we stay connected to Christ, He will enable us to adapt to all of the various, ever-challenging circumstances that we have to deal with. And we will come out on the top and not the bottom. We are the head and not the tail.

Another reminder:

I Corinthians 10:13

"There hath no temptation taken you but such as is common to man: but God is faithful, who will not suffer you to be tempted above that ye are able; but will with the temptation also make a way to escape, that ye may be able to bear it."

Jeremiah 29:11

"For I know the thoughts that I think toward you, says the Lord, thoughts of peace and not evil, to give you a future and a hope."

These are promises that God has made, we just have to live our lives His way. We can trade our peace for His. After all, God planned our journeys and He is working His plan through us.

An example of that is Paul. Before becoming a renowned Apostle, he traveled the land persecuting Christians. After being blinded for days and then healed, he began to preach the Gospel. (Acts 9) As he changed his tune (and name from Saul to Paul) he became a target - being imprisoned (Acts 16) and had people attempt to kill him. In his life, he had gone through a lot; he could have been bitter, upset, or decided to return to his former way of life, but he continued doing what God had placed in his heart to do.

In the midst of this, it is Jesus that is our strongest example, and the One that turned Paul's heart into something fertile and passionate. Jesus went into His life, knowing that He would be laying down His life for the same people who plotted against Him. He knew the pain that He would have to suffer at the hands of those who He was there to save. Even though they mocked Him, spat on Him, and as He looked into the future of the way that His sacrifice would be ignored, forgotten, or manipulated for some to use against others, He still suffered so we wouldn't have to.

Sometimes we have to think of how Jesus would handle these

situations. When we put Him in the forefront of our situation, He will lead and guide us in the right direction; and that is a great peace of mind.

God told us in His Word if we acknowledge Him in all of our ways, He will direct our paths. (Proverbs 3:6)

If we live a Godly life, we will be able to get through everything the enemy brings our way.

Now, we have the power to look at any situation and rebuke it in the name of Jesus. We are conquerors and we will, and can, boldly embrace the life of victory, by the power He has bestowed within us.

He has given us the power to make it through. We just have to hold on to His Word and do it God's Way, not ours.

In this current world, it's very easy to see the easy ways people have prospered and can want to achieve it in a way that we know isn't right. As humans, it's normal for us to feel tempted to be at the middle of the financial frenzy, the glitz and glamour of iniquity, and see how some people profit from others' miseries. Its thrust in our faces due to popular culture, social media, and news outlets, however, it's for us to continue to go down the path that God is leading us.

Galatians 6:9 tells us: "And let us not be weary in well doing: for in due season we shall reap, if we faint not."

I have to remind myself of what He said, and then I can go on and do what He has planned for me to do.

That's why the mantra of "with Christ on my side, nothing can stop me," is so important for staying on a straight path that God has led us on. He is operating His work through us and when we are obedient to what He has told us to do, then He is pleased with us.

Then we can thank God for equipping and empowering us for the victory in this life each and every day. So instead of allowing our thoughts to drag us down, we will allow His Word to build us up.

Where the Finger of God points, the Hand of God leads the way. All we have to do is follow His lead, and not ours. It might seems a little rough sometimes but we know Who is in control. Living God's Way is trading our feet for His.

When we feel like our shoes have worn out, we have a new pair that we can put on today.

All we have to say is: God take the lead of my life and move me out of the way.

Questions

Are you comfortable relying on God to take the lead in your life?

___

Do you trust God to lead you?

___

When God said, " In all your ways acknowledge Him, And He shall direct your paths," what does that mean to you?

___

God is an awesome role model. What kinds of attributes do you feel will make you a good role model?

___

Day 3

Always Rejoice

Philippians 4:4

In this letter to the Philippians, Paul gave an exhortation to rejoice in the Lord always, he even repeated it, "and again, I say Rejoice." (Philippians 4:4)

He was letting them know how important it is to rejoice in the Lord andcontinue to give Him all of the praise, no matter what situation you find yourself in. Rejoice. He wrote this letter while he was in prison in Rome, awaiting trial, but through it all, he continued to rejoice in the Lord.

There's a theory that states that to create a habit, one must do a task 21 times, and then it'll be cemented in their brains. Due to that, we have picked up habits that we've never intended to, and one of those is to relive negativity in our lives. Like a cow that continues to chew the regurgitated cud, many of us are constantly reliving the bad and ignoring the positive things that God has done for us. This could be why Paul had to repeat to us that we should "rejoice," because it's important for us to build a habit out of thanksgiving and joy in the Lord.

That is a great message or command for us as well. We can stand on the promises of God; no matter what the circumstances are, we can stand. He promised never to leave us nor to forsake us. (Hebrews 13:5b) We cannot see Him physically, but Spiritually He is right by our side.

He did not bring us this far to leave us. If we can just think back on how many storms in life He has brought us through, we can rejoice and give Him all of the praise. Not just on Sunday but every day.

In John 16:33, He states to us:

"These things I have spoken unto you, that in Me you will have peace. In the world you will have tribulations; but be of good cheer, I have overcome the world."

Don't be fooled, we will have moments that are going to make us upset, sad, and begin to question our existence, but Jesus reminds us that through it all, we should rejoice in the fact that He has overcome the world. By aligning ourselves with Christ, we have the same power that He has, and know that we too can overcome our circumstances in this world.

Through this we begin to understand the life-changing gift of God through faith in the sacrifice of His Son Jesus. When we truly grasp the concept of eternity and believe we will spend all our days in the presence of God, it's easier to rejoice.

As the song goes "I can only imagine, standing near the Son, to be surrounded by His Glory, for all eternity."

That is enough right there to rejoice in the midst of all of our trials and tribulations that we will face. Because we are children of God, we should not be gloomy but glorious because of our Lord and Savior Jesus Christ.

If we are unable to rejoice while we are going through our trials, all we have to do is turn it over to God and start Rejoicing.

Paul told them in Philippians 4:11, "Not that I speak in respect of want: for I have learned, in whatsoever state I am, therewith to be content." It is a learning process but it can and will happen, all we have to do is keep our mind on Jesus, and we will find ourselves rejoicing.

Paul also told them in Philippians 4:5-6 to "let your [gentleness] be evident to all. The Lord is near. Do not be anxious about anything, but in every situation, by prayer and petition, with thanksgiving, present your request to God." When we give God the praise, thanks, and glory, That is pleasing to Him and He will be pleased with us. But on top of that, it is a testament to those who watch us of the amazing things that God has done and can do for others. We should strive to live a life that is an example to others, and through that, that's how God's grace can touch others, even when our words fall on deaf ears.

Then, He will come forth and show Himself to us in the midst of our circumstances. When He does that, that will transcend all of our understanding, and it will guard our hearts and mind in Christ Jesus. All of the peace He has promised us, hinges on us rejoicing in a Risen Savior.

When we rejoice and focus on eternity in Heaven and our Savior walking by our side, we can't do anything but rejoice. By then, our faith grows stronger and our present trials become light and void.

II Corinthians 4:17-18:

"For our light affliction, which is but for a moment, is working for us a far more exceeding and eternal weight of glory, while we do not look at the things that are seen, but at the things which are not seen. For the things which are seen are temporary, but the things which are not seen are eternal."

That is enough right there to give Him Praise and rejoice in the promises He has made. Our Father has offered us a life of gentleness, contentment, and peace; a life free of anxiety and worry as we seek a refuge in Him.

But this life can only happen if we love and trust Him with all of our heart.

On all of the promises He has made, we are heirs to them all.

Verse 7 of Philippians Chapter 4 reminds us of "And the peace of God, which passeth all understanding, shall keep your hearts and minds through Christ Jesus."

And on that, we will continue and be determined to always rejoice.

In the midst of all trials and tribulation, we can make the choice to continue to regurgitate our negativity into our lives, or to rejoice, because He is our comfort within our storms.

No matter what, we should always rejoice.

Questions

What negative habits do you find that you need to break?

_____
_____
_____
_____

What are everyday things that you can rejoice to God for?

_____
_____
_____
_____

What positive attributes have you noticed in your life once you began to rejoice daily?

_____
_____
_____
_____

What are things that cause you anxiety, and what have you done to purge them from your life?

_____
_____
_____
_____
_____
_____

Day 4

"Sow to Please the Spirit, Not Ourselves"

Galatians 6:7

"...God is not mocked: for whatsoever a man soweth, that shall he also reap."

In the spring, the farmer prepares the soil, plants the seed, and waits several days for the first sign of life for what he has planted. Much hard work and patience goes into a bountiful crop.

The soil of our spirit is rich and full of nutrients with the Word of God.

Every day of our lives we are planting into our spiritual fields.

Each day we are given another opportunity to go into the field and plant new seeds. We are given a choice of which seed to plant. Good or bad.

Sometimes, that can be a difficult choice to make. The enemy is always present and we come up against some trying times.

But we are to sow good seeds, no matter what the situation maybe.

When we do positive things for others, those are favorable seeds that we are sowing. That is what we will reap.

There will be no favoritism. The type of seeds we sow on a daily basis should edify God and not ourselves.

Our actions and speech should be praising God, no matter what. Granted, this is much easier said than done sometimes. As humans, we have emotions, and it's very easy to lend our angry emotions to angry actions and words. But, it's up to us to take control of our actions. We cannot allow others to have power over us, and allow them to take us out of our elements, because each action we make will have a reaction on the garden that we are trying to grow in our lives.

Each day we wake up enclosed in our right mind is another chance to sow good seeds in the ears, mind, and heart of others. No matter where we are, we have the command of God to do His Will and not ours.

Proverbs 18:21 tells us "Death and life are in the power of the tongue: and they that love it shall eat the fruit thereof."

Whether it's on the job, in the grocery store, with family, friends, in the gym, or to our neighbors, each word we utter has the power to build or break down any situation in our lives.

Galatians 6:8 tells us: "For he that soweth to his flesh shall of the flesh reap corruption; but he that soweth to the Spirit shall reap life everlasting.."

In order to reap God's Blessings and all of the promises He has made, we have to make the right choice and He will reward us for our deeds.

Galatians 6:9 tells us: "And let us not be weary in well doing: for in due season we shall reap, if we faint not."

Living a righteous life can be hard. It's a tempting thing to see others seem prosperous by doing things that seem to be unfair. You can watch a person use their tongue to cut a person down and be rewarded by the world. However, the rewards that we seek shouldn't be of the world but from God. Sometimes we might slip up or fall off track. All we have to do is ask for forgiveness and get back on the path of sowing good seeds.

Now, I am not sure of what the time frame of "due season" is, none of us are, but He did say, "We shall reap, if we faint not." This leads me to believe that instead of wondering when our payout will happen, focus on continuing to sow positivity in your life and the lives of others, and God will not forget us.

So this is what we have to do daily; our time is not His time. That is hard sometimes, but we have to stand on His word and not ours, or how we feel about the situation.

I can relate. Sometimes, I just want to sow my own seeds. Sometimes I just want to know when things will prosper for me, and during this time I can feel a strong urge to want to quit. However, it is those times that I remember what God has promised. And that is life everlasting, if we faint not, and that hinges on the two letter word: IF.

John 14:2-3 Jesus tells His Disciples:

"In My Father's house are many mansions; if it were not so, I would have told you. I go to prepare a place for you. And if I go and prepare a place for you, I will come again and receive you to Myself; that where I am, there you may be also."

Then I remind myself that these are not my seeds but God's. On that, I cannot afford to throw in the towel, or drop it for that matter. I want my place that He has prepared for me. We just have to continue to sow good seeds and we will be rewarded.

So as we are sowing seeds, let's be mindful of what type of seeds we are sowing and to whom the seeds belong to in the first place; not us, but God.

We are going to reap what we sow, and our choices do have consequences. I want my sowing to reap what He has promised, and that is Life Everlasting.

So on that, I will sow to please the Spirit and not myself.

Questions

What ways do you sow good seeds in your life?
_____
_____
_____

Any good garden needs to be weeded occasionally. How can you weed your spiritual garden to ensure "healthy fruit?"
_____
_____
_____

What are some good ways to keep yourself motivated when you want to quit?
_____
_____
_____

What areas in your life do you need to sow some prosperous seeds in?
_____
_____
_____

Day 5

"His Calls and Promises Remains"

Romans 11:25-26; 29

"For I would not, brethren, that ye should be ignorant of this mystery, lest ye should be wise in your own conceits; that blindness in part is happened to Israel, until the fullness of the Gentiles be come in.

"And so all Israel shall be saved: as it is written, There shall come out of Sion the Deliverer, and shall turn away ungodliness from Jacob:"

"For the gifts and calling of God *are* without repentance."

When we think about our future, what do we see in our mind's eye?

At one time, we had big goals and dreams, but at a few points in our life we had some disappointments, or life just did not turn out the way we planned it. During these times it can be very easy to give up on the dreams that we had. However, we should not settle for the small things in life, because God's Word tells us God's gifts and plans for our life "are without repentance." (Romans 11:29) Unchangeable, His Word and promises will come to pass.

That's why our life should be, and remain, in the hands of God.

Just because we made some bad choices, He did not give up on us. He knew every mistake we would make, He knew the path we would take, and through it all, He still called us His Children and planned for us to do His Will.

He still designed a perfect plan for our life, no matter what we had planned, His plan for our good still remains.

Joshua 1:9:

"Have not I commanded thee? Be strong and of a good courage; be not afraid, neither be thou dismayed: for the LORD thy God *is* with thee whithersoever thou goest."

That is a strong promise from our God. It was for Joshua, but it still holds true for us today. Since His calling remains, we are going to choose faith over fear.

Faith opens the door for God to work in our lives; fear opens the door for the enemy to do his work.

By operating in faith, we are reaffirming the fact that we still believe in the promises that God has given us, and are going to follow the call He has over our lives. Faith means that we are not going to miss out on God's calling for our lives. His callings are irrevocable. All we have to do is keep the faith and not allow Satan to have any victory in our lives.

Romans 10:17 tells us that: "…faith cometh by hearing, and hearing by the Word of God."

Just like setting the habit of rejoicing in Christ's presence in our lives, we also need to create the habit of hearing the Word. By hearing it and meditating on it daily, we're able to stay in the exceptional mental space of faith. Sometimes we just need to remind ourselves that: "I can do all things through Christ which strengtheneth me." (Philippians 4:13)

So we stand on His Word because it has not and will not change. All we have to do is draw near to Him and He will draw near to us. Then we will be able to feel His strength and joy in our lives. And that is just a reminder that He is still with us.

To this day, His Word has not changed.

He promised that "…I will never leave thee nor forsake thee." (Hebrews 13:5). This promise is just as viable now as it was when it was first uttered, written, and studied throughout the ages. This vow is not just for the ones who first heard it, it's for all who have been blessed to come across it as we made the decision to follow Christ. This is just one more promise we can stand on.

As we are growing more in Faith: Hebrews 11:1 tell us: "Now faith is the substance of things hoped for, the evidence of things not seen."

So when life is not going as we want it to go, we just have to look to the One that is our ALPHA and OMEGA, and ask that His Will be done. We just have to move ourselves out of the way and allow Him to do His work in and through our lives. He planned our lives before we were formed in our mother's womb.

We can't see the end results but we know who has it all in His hand, and that is Christ Jesus Himself.

He is standing by the right hand of the Father pleading our case. So we do not have to worry about the crises of this world.

He is The Great I Am, not The Great I will be, He is The Great I Am now! Psalms 46:1 encourages us with: "God is our refuge and strength, a very present help in trouble." He is waiting for us to give all of our trials and troubles to Him.

One of the steps to achieve is to stir up our faith in Him. His Word remains true. He made the promises a long time ago and they still hold true today. So, since He is our help, who are we to get in the way?

We can keep standing, keep believing and get a vision for our future. In the midst of it all, we can and will grow stronger in our Faith in God and His promises. We do not have to settle for the small things of this life because His Call and His promises Remain.

We are Heirs to all of the promises He made to Abraham. His promises have not and will not change.

They will remain just as He said they would.

Questions

What are some of the promises you feel that God has for your life?

_____
_____
_____

How are you attempting to keep your faith in those promises alive?

_____
_____
_____

Are there any calls from God that you think you are ignoring?

_____
_____
_____

Are you procrastinating on fulfilling your promise to God? If so, why do you think you are doing so?

_____
_____
_____
_____
_____

Day 6

"God Will Not Allow Me to be Stopped"

Jeremiah 29:11-12

"For I know the thoughts that I think toward you, saith the LORD, thoughts of peace, and not evil, to give you an expected end.

Then shall ye call upon me, and ye shall go and pray unto me, and I will hearken unto you."

Each New Year, we spend time planning to make great changes in our lives, and for some, we might try to expect the trials and tribulations that will sometimes come upon us. But, we have the promises of God and all we have to do is believe and trust Him. His word has not and will not change.

In life, we all experience things that are sometimes unexpected. But when trials and tribulations come upon us, and they will come, we have to know that there are no surprises to God. So no matter what comes up into our lives, God is not in the darkness of whatever we may be going through. He is our Alpha and Omega, the beginning and the end of our lives. And that has not changed.

No matter what the New Year may bring or has brought, we have to realize it is no surprise to God. So through it, He will not allow you or your progress to be stopped. The only thing that can stop us are our own actions. If it is up to God, He will always have our side, and He is working to help us win. With that mindset, we should feel free to know that God will always work with us, instead of against us.

You might have lost a loved one, had some changes on the job, but no matter what might have hit you with a surprise, it is no surprise to God.

Sometimes we might say, "I can't believe this is happening," but the Word tell us He knows. But now, since we have been reminded of what God has said and promised us, we can and will have a new perspective on the situation. New Year or not, nothing is new to God.

He has already equipped us to handle it. We know He will not put any more on us than we can bear. He has already anointed us to deal with everything that comes our way. He has given us the strength we need to succeed. And we will, as long as we stay connected to the Vine, and we know the Vine is Jesus Christ our Lord.

The forces that are for us, are much greater than the forces that are against us. Remind yourself of this every New Year; we can and will get through every situation because there are no surprises to God. He promised to give us hope and a future.

We might have been caught off guard but it didn't catch God off guard.

He is ready and prepared to lead us to a place of victory. Our scripture reminded us what He said, that God knows the plans He has for us to help us to prosper. These plans will not harm us but will give us hope and a future.

So all we have to do is keep our trust in Him and He will be right by our side, no matter what, because He promised never to leave us nor forsake us.

His promises for us has not and will not change. Why? Because God is unchangeable.

And we can stand on His Word and continue to trust in Him to go before us and prepare the way for victory in His name.

Numbers 23:19 reminds us that:

"God is not a man, that He should lie; neither the son of man, that He should repent: hath He said, and shall He not do it? Or hath He spoken and shall he not make it good?"

So we can continue to stand on His Word. If He said it, then it is still good today, and we can rest assured that He is working to help us reach the goals that

He promised us and He will not be stopped.

Questions

Do you find that you sabotage God's plan in your life? If so, how?

_____
_____
_____
_____

Were there times when something tried to stop you, but you could feel God working for your benefit?

_____
_____
_____
_____

What are ways that you try to keep yourself encouraged as you follow God's plan for your life?

_____
_____
_____
_____

What are some of the resolutions that you strive to keep each year, and how can you keep them?

_____
_____
_____
_____
_____
_____

Day 7

"Let's Return and Give Thanks"

Luke 17:11-19

"And it came to pass, as He went to Jerusalem, that He passed through the midst of Samaria and Galilee. And as he entered into a certain village, there met him ten men that were lepers, which stood afar off: And they lifted up their voices, and said, Jesus, Master, have mercy on us. And when he saw them, he said unto them, Go shew yourselves unto the priests. And it came to pass, that, as they went, they were cleansed. And one of them, when he saw that he was healed, turned back, and with a loud voice glorified God, And fell down on his face at his feet, giving him thanks: and he was a Samaritan. And Jesus answering said, Were there not ten cleansed? But where are the nine? There are not found that returned to give glory to God, save this stranger. And he said unto him, Arise, go thy way: thy faith hath made thee whole."

Jesus's journey took Him through Samaria and Galilee, headed for the final Passover and His appointment at the Cross.

As he was on His way, He met 10 men that had Leprosy.

Often, they were not accepted by the Jews even though it was some Jews in the group, but when you had Leprosy, you were a castaway.

So they kind of stood off, and when they saw Jesus, they lifted up their voices and said, "Jesus, Master, have Mercy on us."

That is all He wants us to do and all we have to do. They did not go into a long explanation; God knows all about us and what we are going through.

Jesus heard them and told them to go and show themselves to

the Priests.

So they turned around and were obedient to what Jesus told them to do. Sometimes, we have to go on blind faith just as they did.

But as they turned and went on their way, they noticed they were healed.

Just as Jesus heard them call on Him, He will hear us as well. In this day and age, it's sometimes hard to move blindly by faith because there's such a strong emphasis on not only knowing where you're going, but broadcasting it to the world. People rush to make decisions to feel as though they are going somewhere, when in actuality, they are going in the opposite direction that God is leading them. That is what is so interesting about the ten lepers.

Out of the ten, only one turned and went back and with a loud voice glorifying God for his healing, threw himself down at Jesus's feet and said "thank you."

Jesus took the time out of His scheduled trip and healed these men. He will do the same for us at any given time - day or night.

Now all of them were healed, but only one said thank you. He has taken time to heal us and listen to our cry. He has heard us and satisfied us according to His Will.

He has taken the time to heal us physically and spiritually. He has dispatched His angels to be around us to keep us safe. He has given us a place to sleep and food to eat and so on.

How many times have we received God's Blessings and did not say thank you?

We made it here today safe and without harm by His traveling Grace. When I see a car accident on the side of the street, I say "Lord, I thank You; that could have been me."

Then when I make it back home, everything is like I left it, I say, "Lord, I thank you."

There is a luxury in routine, and not predictability. When we go to our jobs, stores to shop, or our normal errand destinations, and then come back home and nothing has burned down or been stolen; it's easy to take it for granted. However, those multiple times of uneventful runnings were blessed by God's Hand. He kept us safe while we were out, watched over our homes and loved ones who are still alive when we call them. Because it wasn't a seemingly miraculous event, we can be blind to how bless we are to our routine. When in actuality, God could have been protecting us from many dangers that we didn't know.

In the eye sight of God, we should not want to be like the ten that kept going and did not stop and say thank you. Even in the most seemingly banal moments, we should always thank God because He is protecting us during those times, as well as the ones that are disastrous.

Ephesians 2:4-5 tells us: But God, who is rich in mercy, for his great love wherewith he loved us, Even when we were dead in sins, hath quickened us together with Christ, (by grace ye are saved)…

Just as the one went back and praised Jesus with a loud voice, that is what we should do as well, because even when we are doing wrong, His mercy is on us.

He continues to heal and deliver. That is truly the love of God. When we wandered off and did our own thing, He did not leave us alone. He kept His loving arms around us.

Because He did not leave us in our mess, with a loud voice we should say thank You, and give Him the Honor and the Glory for all He has done in our lives.

When we realize that we did not get to this point in our lives all by ourselves, we should be like the one Leper, just turn ourselves around and say Thank You.

Thank You.

Questions

What every day events are blessings for you?

_____
_____
_____
_____

Have there been moments when you realized that God protected you from something horrible? (For example: taking a different route, only to realize that there was a large accident on your original route that you could have potentially been harmed in.)

_____
_____
_____
_____

What daily blessings keep you motivated to continue to thank God?

_____
_____
_____
_____

Do you find it better to thank God at the beginning of the day, the end, or both? Why?

_____
_____
_____
_____

Day 8

"Each Day I will Humble Myself, Create and Renew My Spirit with Christ"

Psalms 51:1-3; 10-11

"(To the chief Musician, A Psalm of David, when Nathan the prophet came unto him, after he had gone in to Bath-sheba.) Have mercy upon me, O God, according to thy lovingkindness: according unto the multitude of thy tender mercies blot out my transgressions. Wash me thoroughly from mine iniquity, and cleanse me from my sin. For I acknowledge my transgressions: and my sin is ever before me.

"Create in me a clean heart, O God; and renew a right spirit within me. Cast me not away from thy presence; and take not thy holy spirit from me."

In Psalms 51:1-3 Nathan, the prophet, went in to talk to David after he had committed adultery with Bathsheba. She had become pregnant and David put her husband Uriah on the front line of battle and he was killed.

After God sent Nathan in to talk to David, his sins were brought before him, he fell to his knees and cried out to God for forgiveness.

After David did this awful thing, he was very sorrowful in his heart. Now, the guilt sets in.

When the guilt of our lives set in, it will bring us to our knees to ask for forgiveness.

David, in Psalms 51:10-11 cries out to God, saying:

"Create in me a clean heart, O God; and renew a right spirit within me.

Cast me not away from thy presence; and take not thy holy spirit from me."

Here David was making it personal. He used the word "me." He was not praying a generic prayer, he was calling it just as it was.

That's what we need to do - confess our sins to God. We shouldn't take advantage of the fact that God knows what we did. In order to be truly forgiven, we must humble ourselves, admit our faults, and become emotionally bare to the Father. In the same way if you're at a doctor, they will disrobe you to treat your ailments, that's what God needs us to do. He needs us to remove our cloak of wrongs and become vulnerable so we can not only be healed, but learn from our mistakes.

Here David is saying I acknowledge my transgressions, and my sin is ever before me. God knew David was going to do what he did, but David was still responsible for being knowledgeable about the wrongs he committed.

Verse 4 tells us: "Against thee, thee only, have I sinned, and done this evil in thy sight: that thou mightest be justified when thou speakest, and be clear when thou judgest."

Here David is doing what we have to do: make a confession and ask God to "Create in me a clean heart, O God; and renew a right spirit within me."

We have made mistakes along the way as well, just as David did. No Matter what our sins may be, they will not dissipate until we ask God to purge us, make us clean, and forgive us.

According to Psalms 25:7, David said, "Remember not the sins of my youth, nor my transgressions: according to thy mercy remember thou me for thy goodness' sake, O Lord."

If we fail to give our sins to God, then we will end up empty and defeated.

When we feel as though we have been broken, then we are where

God wants us to be. He wants us to give all of our pain and hurt to Him, and He is there for us time and time again.

He is the only One that can heal and repair our brokenness. Pride has to be pushed aside here; humility has to be set in.

Here David is praying for his inner renewal. He asked that God not take His Spirit away from him. We can be just as David was when he asked God for a Spiritual renewing.

We know when we are not right, our bodies are the Temple of the Holy Spirit and He lets us know immediately, and all we have to do is repent of our wrongdoings and ask God to renew the right Spirit within us.

No matter what is going on around us, or within us, He can and will wash us and make us clean.

As Paul was writing to the Romans in Romans 12:1-2, He told them:

"I beseech you therefore, brethren, by the mercies of God, that ye present your bodies a living sacrifice, holy, acceptable unto God, [which is] your reasonable service.

And be not conformed to this world: but be ye transformed by the renewing of your mind, that ye may prove what [is] that good, and acceptable, and perfect, will of God."

First he said to present our bodies, and then he said to prove it. In order to do so, we must actively go in front of the Father during these times of asking for forgiveness. It's not enough to just think it, but we have to actually pray and admit our wrongdoings in a moment of sincerity.

Even though He dwells on the inside of us, it is not always easy. But that is what He expects of us. Sometimes we fall down but He is able to pick us up again and again.

We are all like David, we've done some things that was not pleasing to God, but we are forgiven by His Grace and Mercy. He can create within us a clean heart, and renew the right Spirit within us. It is ours for the asking.

Questions

Is there anything that you need to ask God's forgiveness for?

_____
_____
_____

Do you have a problem forgiving others?

_____
_____
_____

How do you think salvation would work if God treated forgiveness like we sometimes do?

_____
_____
_____

What is the hardest thing you've ever had to forgive someone for?

_____
_____
_____

If we didn't ask for forgiveness, and carried all of our sins with us, how hard would it be to maintain a strong Christian walk?

_____
_____
_____

Day 9

"I will Seek Comfort in Trusting God"

John 14:13-18

"And whatsoever ye shall ask in my name, that will I do, that the Father may be glorified in the Son.

If ye shall ask any thing in my name, I will do it.

If ye love me, keep my commandments.

And I will pray the Father, and he shall give you another Comforter, that he may abide with you for ever;

Even the Spirit of truth; whom the world cannot receive, because it seeth him not, neither knoweth him: but ye know him; for he dwelleth with you, and shall be in you.

I will not leave you comfortless: I will come to you."

When we feel like we are at the end of our rope, we need a reminder, of who is really at the end of the Rope. It is Jesus Christ Himself.

He is the Counselor that God promised to send us, and He is standing in the gap for us. He is the deposit that has been installed within us, and we can withdraw and reap the benefits anytime we need to. All we have to do is ask in His name. He promised not to leave us comfortless. He said He would come to us. That is a promise we can stand on.

Sometimes we don't know what to say in our prayers as we should, but

Romans 8:26 says: "...The Spirit also helpeth our infirmities: for we know not what we should pray for as we ought: but the Spirit itself makes intercession for us with groanings which cannot be uttered."

This is basically telling us that we don't have to use overly flowery words to talk to God, all we have to do is talk. Our Spirit knows exactly how to get our words across to Him so that He knows exactly what we want to say.

The fact that He is standing in the gap for us, that is a tremendous blessing within itself.

After we let our hearts be known, He will take all of our hurts, disappointments, and needs, whatever we are going through, He will take all of them to the Father. After all, He took all of our cares to the cross, so He knows what we are going through. He will not allow us to go through anything that He has not gone through. We just have to stay connected to Jesus Christ, because the only way to the Father is through Him.

2 Corinthians 4:8-9;16 tells us:

"We are troubled on every side, yet not distressed; we are perplexed, but not in despair; persecuted, but not forsaken; cast down, but not destroyed;"

"For which cause we faint not; but though our outward man perish, yet the inward man is renewed day by day."

We just have to trust and believe God. We have faith in our Lord and Savior Jesus Christ, which is a treasure that we have in these earthly vessels.

We have to know that the Excellence of the power is of God and not us.

When He is doing a work within us, we have to be still and allow Him to do His Will through us, and then give Him all of the credit.

We cannot do anything without God. He is the Author and the Finisher of our faith. Whatever we want, if it is written in His Word and if it is His Will for us, all we have to do is ask and it will come to pass. His Word is still true today and will always be true.

If we put our trust in God, all of our needs will be met. That is the comfort that He promised to us.

Sometimes our days seem dark and dim. Sometimes, we cannot see our way:

But Psalms 94:18-19 affirms to us:

"When I said, "my foot is slipping", your unfailing love, Lord, supported me.

When anxiety was great within me, your consolation brought me joy." NIV

Isaiah 40:29-31 tells us:

"He giveth power to the faint; and to them that have no might He increaseth strength.

Even the youths shall faint and be weary, and the young men shall utterly fall:

But they that wait upon the Lord shall renew their strength; they shall mount up with wings as eagles; they shall run, and not be weary; and they shall walk, and not faint."

If we keep our trust in Christ Jesus and faint not, we will be comforted beyond measure. He did not bring us this far to leave us, nor forsake us.

All we have to do is stay connected and He will deliver all of the promises He made, and He will comfort us, just as He said He would.

Proverbs 3:1-6:

"My son, forget not my law; but let thine heart keep my commandments:

For length of days, and long life, and peace, shall they add to thee."

Let not mercy and truth forsake thee: bind them about thy neck; write them upon the table of thine heart:

So shalt thou find favour and good understanding in the sight of God and man.

Trust in the Lord with all thine heart; and lean not unto thine own understanding. In all thy ways acknowledge Him, and He shall direct thy paths."

All of the peace and comfort He promised us, we will reap because He said, "because I live, ye shall live also." Here are a few more scriptures to keep you encouraged and comfort you as you go through your daily walk, face tribulations, or just feel down. These will remind you that you can trust in God's ability to be there for us.

Nahum 1:7:

"The Lord is good, a strong hold in the day of trouble; and He knoweth them that trust in Him."

Psalms 27:14

"Wait on the Lord: be of good courage, and He shall strengthen thine heart: wait, I say, on the Lord."

There is Comfort in trusting the Lord.

Questions

What times do you feel as though you need the most comfort?

_____
_____
_____
_____

Think back to a time that you were stressed out and you called out to God, how did He comfort you then?

_____
_____
_____
_____

God will bless us with certain talents; what talents and hobbies of yours do you go to receive comfort?

_____
_____
_____
_____

Is there a practice you can do daily to remind yourself of God's comfort?

_____
_____
_____
_____
_____

Day 10

"I Will Deny My Flesh, and Carry My Cross Daily"

II Corinthians 4:17-18

"For our light affliction, which is but for a moment, worketh for us a far more exceeding and eternal weight of glory;

While we look not at the things which are seen, but at the things which are not seen: for the things which are seen are temporal; but the things which are not seen are eternal."

The path of a successful Christian walk is one of a daily commitment to Christ and submission to the leading of the Holy Spirit.

Jesus said in Luke 9:23: "…If any man will come after me, let him deny himself, and take up his cross daily, and follow me."

What does he mean when he expresses this to us?

As anyone who is familiar with Jesus's crucifixion knows, not only was that a hard task for Jesus, but the anticipation of it gave Him anxiety.

In Luke 22:42 and 44, Jesus expresses to God that:

"…if thou be willing, remove this cup from me: nevertheless not my Will, but Thine, be done." "And being in an agony He prayed more earnestly: and his sweat was as it were great drops of blood falling falling down to the ground."

It is very evident that Jesus was in turmoil over the pain that awaited Him. On top of that, to be able to know that even after performing this incredible act of love, there were going to be people who would curse Him, deny Him, and insult Him from that moment, to the present, to the future. However, He knew that in order for salvation to become a choice for all, He had to sacrifice

Himself. In that sense, He took on His own cross, as an example to us that making sacrifices are going to be hard, but necessary, while following the path that God has for us.

This is true for us Christians as well.

Paul understood this commitment when he said in 1 Corinthians 15:31: "...I die daily."

2 Corinthians 4:16 says, "For which cause we faint not; but though our outward man perish, yet the inward man is renewed day by day."

Each and every day we are faced with something that could lead us to either feed into our flesh, or deny it by following the path God has for us. Our flesh is that little voice/urge/impulse that wants us to do something that is not of God; whether it is allowing our anger to get the best of us, following idle desires, or willingly falling into temptation. These things, that might feel satisfying in the moment, are out of the Will of God and will place space between us and our Savior. The Bible lets us know that sin is something that separates us from God (Isaiah 59:2), and following our flesh, is going down the path toward sin. Essentially, indulging in sin is easy, but doing what's right always takes an extra, concerted effort and requires some form of sacrifice that might end up hurting us.

For example, the other day, someone took the parking space that I was waiting for, but rather give Satan the victory and get upset, I just said, "Lord, I thank You that I am able to walk a little further." It would have been very easy to curse at the driver, or put up a middle finger to get the point across, but it took effort to find the positive in the situation, and that's what I did. Just as Paul said, we are faced with something every day, but the good news is that, with anything, if you practice at it, it gets easier.

All we have to do is tell Satan that he has no victory here.

Rebuke him in the name of Jesus. When we do that, victory is on the way.

We can see our old nature has died when our heart was transformed by the Spirit of God. Yet there remains an on-going task of pruning as we continue our walk and battle the temptations from a world which seeks to pull us away from God.

When He prunes us, He takes the very desires of worldly things from us. When the desires of the world come upon us, all we have to do is give it all to Jesus, and He will get us through everything Satan brings our way.

This is where we need to weigh the odds and ask ourselves a question: Is this worth me losing all the promises God has promised me? At that time in our life, we need to make it personal, just us and God.

Our daily commitment and denials can be painful sometimes, but we have to focus on our present circumstances and ask ourselves a powerful question: Is this worth it?

We have to weigh the odds; we are looking for peace and joy eternally. He has promised us no more tears, no more pain, no more disappointments, but joy and peace.

So no matter what we are going through, we have to remember what He said in His Word. Paul expressed this in Philippians 1:21 as he shared: "...to live is Christ, and to die is gain."

In Matthew 16:25, it is written: "For whosoever will save his life shall lose it: and whosoever will lose his life for my sake shall find it."

Jesus is telling us about the sacrifices that He is expecting us to make each day while we go down our own chosen paths. Jesus, though He warns us of the potential peril, He let's us know that there's joy on the other side. He is showing compassion for us.

He said in John 16:33:

"These things I have spoken unto you, that in Me ye might have peace. In the world ye shall have tribulation: but be of good cheer;

I have overcome the world."

He also assures us that He would not allow anything to come upon us that we cannot bear, or that He did not go through (I Corinthians 10:13). He overcame the world for us, so we could put our lives on the scale of eternal life.

Here's what we need to remember - God is not promising us a life without pain, because the world is fallen and in torment, which means that we will have moments of tribulations. However, Psalms 34:19 assures us that: "Many are the afflictions of the righteous: but the Lord will delivereth him out of them all."

That is why we have to stay connected to the Vine, and we know the Vine is Jesus Christ Himself.

He did all of this for us.

Since He did this for us, now the burdens that were once heavy in our lives, can be weighed against the promises of Eternal life with Jesus Christ.

Now we look at God's promise of eternal life. When trials and tribulations come into our lives, we can put our lives on the scale of Eternal life with Jesus Christ.

We should focus on the here and now, and definitely not the past or too much into the future. There's a popular internet phrase that dictates that: "If you live in the past, you're depressed. If you live in the future, you're anxious. However, if you live in the present, you're at peace."

James 4:14 tells us that our earthly life is short, like a mist that appears for a short while, and then vanishes away.

So we do not have time to dwell on the mishaps that come upon us, all we have to do is give it to God, and He will handle it each and every time.

Don't think that God doesn't know what it means to worry, because it must have been a struggle to send His own Son to a fate that would cause Him pain. However, God did it for us, like expressed in John 3:16: "For God so loved the world, that He gave His only begotten Son, that whosoever believeth in Him should not perish, but have everlasting life."

That is another promise He made to, and for us, so when we put our lives on the scales of what we want and what God has promised, we will come out on the winning side.

His promises has and will not change. On that, I want the good in my life to outweigh the bad.

He promised life for eternity and that is what we will have in the name of Jesus.

Questions

What is something you struggle with daily?

_____
_____
_____
_____

How do you attempt to deny your flesh when it concerns that daily struggle?

_____
_____
_____
_____

Since God offers us grace when we make a mistake, how do you give yourself grace?

_____
_____
_____
_____

Are there any other things in your life that you feel like you need to give up to please God?

_____
_____
_____
_____

How do some of your repeated sins separate you from God?

_____
_____
_____
_____

Day 11

"I will put on the garment of Praise"

Ephesians 6:10-17

"Finally, my brethren, be strong in the Lord, and in the power of his might. Put on the whole armour of God, that ye may be able to stand against the wiles of the devil. For we wrestle not against flesh and blood, but against principalities, against powers, against the rulers of the darkness of this world, against spiritual wickedness in high *places*. Wherefore take unto you the whole armour of God, that ye may be able to withstand in the evil day, and having done all, to stand. Stand therefore, having your loins girt about with truth, and having on the breastplate of righteousness; And your feet shod with the preparation of the gospel of peace; Above all, taking the shield of faith, wherewith ye shall be able to quench all the fiery darts of the wicked. And take the helmet of salvation, and the sword of the Spirit, which is the word of God:"

After we get out of bed, we start our day by getting dressed and we move on to whatever we have to do. As we are planning our day, we dress for the occasion, but are we dressed for the enemy as well?

We are blessed to have a choice of outfits to choose from. We've read God's instructions as to what to put on and to take off. Each day we face the enemy in some way or another. To help us dress for the Biblical weather, God encourages us to, "Put on the whole armor of God." However, for it to be effective, we must wear the whole ensemble. He did not say make sure it matches your shoes, jewelry or anything else, He just said put it on.

As our day progresses, we come in contact with the enemy; it might be on the job, at the stoplight, in the grocery store, or in our home.

There is no place where the enemy is not present, that's why we have to be prepared each and every day. His job is to steal, kill, and destroy (John 10:10), so that is why we need to be dressed for the battle every minute of the day.

No matter what He allows us to go through, He has a promise and a plan already in place for us. All we have to do is stay connected to our Lord and Savior Jesus Christ, and stay dressed for the battle. When we look back in retrospect on our lives, we can see the love God has shown for us.

The same promise that God made to Moses, who imparted that truth to Joshua, we know that God will never leave us, nor forsake us (Deuteronomy 31:8). That promise is still upheld to this day. We can stand and depend on His Word. Because of that, we need to be dressed for the battle and not ourselves.

One thing He said that's very important is to "Put on the whole armor...," he never said take it off. So we are to keep the armor on morning, noon, and night. He is telling us to be prepared at all times.

The life of our soldiers at war is very difficult. They live under a constant threat of attack. Each day they must prepare for battle. Each day they must dress to face the enemy. Just as they have to be prepared for the attack of the enemy, we have to do the same.

There will be times when we go through some hard times, but His Word has reminded me that He is "the lifter up of mine head" (Psalm 3:3) time and time again.

Then Paul said in Ephesians 6:10, "Finally, my brethren, be strong in the Lord, and in the power of His might."

We have to be strong in the Lord. When we learn the Word of God, we have to put some action behind it; and when we do our part, God will do the rest. We have to put on the whole armor of God, not just what we want to put on, but the entire armor of God. Only then will that allow us to be able to stand against the wiles of the devil.

Satan comes in so many ways and from so many directions. That's why we have to have the whole armor on at all times.

When we are going through our storms of life, He told us "…the battle is not yours, but God's," in 2 Chronicles 20:15.

But when we stand on the Word of God, having our loins girded with the truth and having on the breastplate of righteousness, when we follow all of God's rules, we will be able to quench all the fiery darts of the wicked.

We know the helmet of salvation and the sword of the Spirit is the Word of God. When we are dressed with the whole armor, the enemy will have no victory.

Satan is determined to steal our joy and cause us to be ineffective soldiers on the battlefield for the Lord.

Even though we know that if we stay focused and in our armor, God makes no allusions of frivolity in this spiritual war. He did not tell us the battle would be easy, but He promised to be there for us. He knows what we are going through and He will not leave us, nor forsake us. That is another promise we can stand on.

All we have to do is put God first, He will be there for us to fight the battle.

So as we enter each day, let's fight bravely and dress as He said to dress, with the whole armor on. Sometimes we might have to ask the Lord to bridle our tongues, and He will do that as well.

Only then will we be able to stand, walk and talk in the name of Jesus Christ, and we will let the enemy know he has no victory here. We should be dressed for the battle each and every day.

There will be times when we might feel mentally fatigued, but Paul also said in Ephesians 6:10: "Finally, my brethren, be strong in the Lord, and in the Power of His might." Remember that we are fighting this battle, not on our own strength and merits, but through the power of Jesus Christ.

Questions

What is a piece of God's armor that is easy for you to use?

_____
_____
_____

What is a piece of armor that you need help remembering to use?

_____
_____
_____

How can you strengthen yourself in that armor?

_____
_____
_____

If you were to go to war today, would you be ready, and why?

_____
_____
_____

What is another way to keep your mind vigil on the spiritual war?

_____
_____
_____
_____

Day 12

"I am Becoming Complete"

Philippians 1:3-6

"I thank my God upon every remembrance of you, Always in every prayer of mine for you all making request with joy, For your fellowship in the gospel from the first day until now; Being confident of this very thing, that he which hath begun a good work in you will perform it until the day of Jesus Christ:"

We all have dreams and visions for our lives. Sometimes we wait and wait for them to come to pass. We pray and then wait even more.

We find ourselves standing on the promises of God but sometimes it seems as though God has forgotten about us. We know He has not because He promised us never to leave us nor to forsake us.

Becoming complete does not happen overnight. It actually starts the moment we accept Christ in our hearts as our Savior and Lord.

Philippians 1:6 reminded me that He said being confident [in the Lord], He who began a good work in you, will continue to perform it, until it is perfectly complete.

Also, Hebrews 10:35 states: "Cast not away therefore your confidence, which hath great recompense of reward."

Our timeline is different from God's time, His ways are different from our ways. But He is a God of completion. He will finish what He has started in our lives. He is also our Alpha and Omega. The beginning and the end. When we think He has forgotten about us and our needs, He is working behind the scenes on our behalf. He is truly the Author and Finisher of our Faith. As Paul stated, "...a good work in you will perform it until the day of Jesus Christ:".

We will not be complete until the coming of Christ Himself. So when we feel as though we have been left behind, He is still in the forefront of our lives. We just have to get our lives and minds off of worldly things and continue to look to Him and keep standing on His Word. After all, if He said it, it will come to pass.

He can and will do His work through us. So let's not give up, sometimes God allows us to go through things so we will have a testimony to help others come to know who Jesus Christ really is. He is working His work through us.

Phil. 1:29: "For unto you it is given in the behalf of Christ, not only to believe on Him, but also to suffer for His sake;". When we go through our storms of life, we come out stronger. We know it was no one but God. We just have to remember that He is the comfort in the midst of our storms.

We want to live a life so that others can see the Christ in us. After all, Jesus is our role model, and we do not want to bring any shame to His name.

Even though He is not through with us yet, we will be complete upon His return. As long as we keep our faith and trust in Him and stay connected to the vine, that is a promise we can stand on.

With sincere trust in God, we do not have to ponder on things that we think are big issues. We need to think on how Big Our God is. God is showing us His love each and every day. As long as we keep our mind and heart stayed on Him, He will bring all of His promises to pass.

With each and every testimony we have, that is building our unshakeable confidence in Him even more until His Word and command will be complete.

Questions

What are ways that you can be a living testimony for Christ without using words?

_____
_____
_____
_____

What is a testimony you have for when you waited on God's time rather than going on your own?

_____
_____
_____
_____

When your confidence is low, what is a way to strengthen it in following God's commandment for your life?

_____
_____
_____
_____

What works are you doing to complete God's path for your life?

_____
_____
_____
_____

Are there any bad habits you need to break to keep you on God's course?

_____
_____
_____
_____

Day 14

"I will be Pliable for the Potter's Hand"

Jeremiah 18:1-6

"The word which came to Jeremiah from the LORD, saying, Arise, and go down to the potter's house, and there I will cause thee to hear my words. Then I went down to the potter's house, and, behold, he wrought a work on the wheels. And the vessel that he made of clay was marred in the hand of the potter: so he made it again another vessel, as seemed good to the potter to make it. Then the word of the LORD came to me, saying, O house of Israel, cannot I do with you as this potter? saith the LORD. Behold, as the clay is in the potter's hand, so are ye in mine hand, O house of Israel."

Jeremiah was commanded to go to the potter's house in order to learn a lesson. The potters house was probably located in the southern section of the city, or perhaps in the potter's field south of Jerusalem, just beyond the valley of Hinnom.

The wheels were two circular stones connected by a vertical shaft. The potter could sit at the wheel, spinning the lower stone with his feet and causing the upper disc to rotate. This enables both hands to be free in order to work the clay. Should the vessel become marred or any impurity detected, the potter would not discard the clay, but simply remold it into another vessel.

No matter how broken we might feel our lives are, God is the potter and we are the clay. He can make, shape, and mold us into His likeness at any time He chooses. All we have to do is ask.

God taught the Prophet Jeremiah what it meant to be a Sovereign God.

He taught him that God's plan would be fulfilled one way or the other.

Either his children would submit to gentle guidance, or He would bring discipline to teach them the need for obedience. God does have the last word over our lives.

So that leaves a question for us: "where do we stand?"

We all fall short of God's perfection. We can ask to be put back on the Potter's Wheel, if we truly want to be made perfect in His Will. We are like the clay in the hands of the potter.

Romans 3:23 tells us, "...All have sinned, and come short of the glory of God." Therefore, we are all masses filled with imperfection. Though we might feel as though we aren't useable, God still has the ability to mold us. We can ask to be reshaped and molded so that we can be made perfect in His image.

Though the Potter has a work to do, there's still work on our own part. Even in our flaws, we must submit to the Potter, and turn away from our former behavior. If we do not repent and turn from our evil ways, just as God told Jeremiah to tell the people that, "I will scatter them as with an east wind before the enemy; I will shew them the back, and not the face, in the day of their calamity."

We do not want God to turn His face from us. At certain times, we just need to be put back on the potter's wheel.

We can ask that everything that is unlike Him, be removed from our lives, and when He takes it away, we should ask Him not to leave us void but fill that emptiness with more of His love, grace and Holy Spirit.

He told Jeremiah that: "if that nation, against whom I have pronounced, turn from their evil, I will repent of the evil that I thought to do unto them."

So what does that mean for us?

When we repent and ask for forgiveness, we should turn from doing the things that please us and turn to pleasing God. We can ask to be put back on the potter's wheel to be made whole again.

Jeremiah understood that God was the Potter and He had control of the shape of the clay. How foolish would it be to complain or rebel, since we are the clay in the Potter's hand, which is God's hand? All we have to do is ask that we be made over, in His likeness, and not ours.

The Potter will continue to mold the clay. But if the clay gets hard before it is complete, while it is in an unfinished state, He will crush it down and sprinkle it with water and start over again. Sometimes, if and when we do not listen to His calling on our lives, He will allow us to be crushed, in order for us to be raised up again.

The only way for us to become all that God desires us to be is to yield and remain pliable. We have no ability to shape ourselves. We are being shaped and molded in the likeness of His Son Jesus.

Romans 8:29 states, "For whom he did foreknow, he also did predestinate to be conformed to the image of His Son, that he might be the firstborn among many brethren." All we have to do is ask.

Sometimes, when we think we got it all together, that's when we need to give it over to God. There are times we might have a few rough edges that need to be removed. However, in our own hands, we might think that it's okay, but in reality, it's cutting the hands we use to mold ourselves. That's when His reshaping process will take place. We have to remain moldable clay and yield our lives to the shaping of the potters hand.

Jesus did not come to make God's love possible but to make His love visible. He came and gave His life for us, the least we can do, is give our lives back to Him.

When we allow ourselves to be put back on the potter's wheel, then we can be that light that sits on a hill so others will see the working of God in our lives.

In essence, we are like David when he said in Psalms 51:7-12:

"Purge me with hyssop, and I shall be clean: wash me, and I shall be whiter than snow. Make me hear joy and gladness; that the bones which thou hast broken may rejoice. Hide thy face from my sins and blot out all mine iniquities.

Create in me a clean heart, O God; and renew a right spirit within me. Cast me not away from thy presence; and take not thy Holy Spirit from me.

Restore unto me the joy of thy salvation; and uphold me with thy free spirit."

I ask Him to shape me and mold me in His Image and not mine.

He is the Potter and I am the clay!

Questions

What times do you notice that you try to mold yourself?

_____
_____
_____
_____

When was a time that molding yourself failed?

_____
_____
_____
_____

What are ways to keep you pliable for God's molding?

_____
_____
_____
_____

What are some of your imperfections that God has turned for His Good?

_____
_____
_____
_____
_____

What are some of your imperfections that you feel need to be purged?

_____
_____
_____
_____
_____

How can you keep yourself patient while being molded by God?

Day 15

"I will plant imperishable seeds"

Isaiah 55:8-11

"For my thoughts are not your thoughts, neither are your ways my ways, saith the LORD. For as the heavens are higher than the earth, so are my ways higher than your ways, and my thoughts than your thoughts. For as the rain cometh down, and the snow from heaven, and returneth not thither, but watereth the earth, and maketh it bring forth and bud, that it may give seed to the sower, and bread to the eater: So shall my word be that goeth forth out of my mouth: it shall not return unto me void, but it shall accomplish that which I please, and it shall prosper in the thing whereto I sent it."

In reading this passage, this question came to me: are we not accountable to plant the seed of God in others? After all, how many seeds have been planted with us?

When we are connected with Jesus Christ, it is hard not to sow good seeds. He compared His Word with the rain and the snow. As we look at the grass and trees, which is God's Word working within them, No one is watering those large trees, but they are still growing because He said His Word will not go out and return unto Him void. The rain and the snow are for a reason, though we might not always understand it. Our ways and thoughts are not His.

If you look at the seasons, we have moments of flourish in the earth, and then winter comes along and seemingly kills our local vegetation. The leaves from trees fall and crumble, leaving the branches barren. Flowers wilt due to the cold, and grass turns brown. We might wonder, why have such a season if it only brings destruction? However, each spring, those same plants and trees flourish, and they could only be going through a period of cold that allowed them to lose some of their dead weight so they can regrow bigger and grander.

As we look back over our lives we can see that seeds were planted within us, it might have taken a while for them to take root and grow, but they did, and some are still growing, just as The Word said they would. Even though we might go through periods of winter where things seem rough, we should always remember that spring will come soon and allow us to flourish.

Someone planted, someone watered, but God did the increase. That is the Word of God doing what He said He would do. He said His Word would not go out and return unto Him void. And now we can see the results in our own lives. Even though we did not see it at the time, but now, in retrospect, we know seeds were planted in our lives.

When we have a chance to witness or testify to others, we are only to say what thus said the Word of God. Not what we think, or want to say, but what God said in His Word. His Word will come to pass - not ours.

We could be the ones that are doing the watering, or planting; we don't know. God is using us to reach His people. He is speaking through us. That's why we have to keep ourselves in line with Jesus and His Word.

He did not tell us to hang around to see the end results. He just said do it. If we do our part, He will send someone else to that same situation. We don't know if we are planting or watering, but we know who will do the increase. Just as His Word said He would do.

Verse 11 says: "but [my Word] shall accomplish that which I please, and it shall prosper in the things whereto I sent it."

So, our witness is not about us, it is all about Jesus and Him alone. That is why we have to keep our lives on His path so that He can - and will - use us for His purpose. God promised to keep us lifted up and in His care, as long as we keep our mind, hope and faith in Him. It is truly a blessing to be used by God.

When He sees enough favor in us, to reach His people, I do not take that for granted at all. When we do our part, then our growth will increase and He will use us again and again to plant His Seed in the hearts of His people.

We are called to encourage one another. In Hebrews 10:25 we're told: "not forsaking the assembling of ourselves together…" We are to just plant the seed of encouragement when He tells us to; He will do the increase. The end results are in His hand. Not only to the brothers and sisters that are in Christ, we are to share the Word with the ones that do not know the Lord and His Word.

Jesus was not always in the Temple. He was among the ones that needed Him as their Lord and Savior. He went out into the World and talked, taught, and touched those around Him. His Words weren't just for the people in the church, but for those who didn't go to church, and for those who didn't even know where the church was.

Many people are walking in a spiritually dry land and we may be the only bit of Jesus that they will see, hear or read. He told us to be that light that sits on a hill so that others will see. That is planting good seeds in the sight of men.

We do not know how, when, or where God is going to use us. But, when He uses us, we are to plant His seed and not ours. We are to freely cast out seeds and the refreshing water of His Word and trust that He will do just what He said He would do.

After all, growth is in the hands of God, so we are simply workers that are planting the seed of God. However, we are responsible for the type of seed we are planting. We should only plant Good seed, and that is The Word of God.

Jesus said in John 3:3, "…Verily, verily, I say unto thee, Except a man be born again, he cannot see the Kingdom of God."

That is why we are to plant good seeds along the way. Those seeds will result in Eternal Life, and that is Life Ever Lasting, in the presence of Jesus Christ our Savior.

God has placed seeds of greatness inside of us, and our duty to God is to plant those seeds inside of others. Whether it is planting or watering, we are to be obedient to God's Word.

Some seeds take longer to germinate than others, but God will do the increase in His perfect time. Sometimes we can feel as though we are failing because the person is in a spiritual winter, but God knows when the spring bounty will burst forward. He has a plan already laid out for us all.

So let's plant a true message of God by always being obedient to His Word and not ours.

That is what He has told us to do - to plant His seed and not ours.

Questions

How do you actively plant seeds in people's lives?

_____
_____
_____
_____

In what ways do your actions plant seeds?

_____
_____
_____
_____

What was a seed that someone planted in you, and how did they do it (by words or actions?)?

_____
_____
_____
_____

Write about a time of spiritual winter, then of spiritual spring.

_____
_____
_____
_____

Have you ever had a moment when someone noticed your actions when you didn't realize you were being watched? How did the resulting revelation make you feel?

_____
_____
_____
_____

Day 16

"God Is my Refuge and my Strength"

Psalms 46:10-11

"Be still, and know that I am God: I will be exalted among the heathen, I will be exalted in the earth. The LORD of hosts is with us; the God of Jacob is our refuge. Selah."

The word refuge means, "A place of safety, place of protection, or shelter." When things are not going as they should, we don't have to worry; God is here for us, right now. He said, "[I am a] very present help in trouble." (Psalms 46:1) He said a present help, meaning, right now. He also said, "Be still, and know that I am God:".

God is an all-knowing God. He knows what's going to happen even before we find ourselves in the middle of a travesty. He knows my issues, He knows yours as well. He has all of them worked out already. We just have to wait on God's time. Remember what He said: "Be still" and "wait."

God is our refuge and strength, a present help in times of trouble. With our trust and belief in God, we can see the results with our spiritual eye before we can see it with our natural eye.

He is looking down, and He is watching all of us at the same time. He is everything that we could ever want or need. Again, when we think we are at the end of our rope, we just need a reminder of who is really at the end of that rope.

It is Jesus Christ Himself. He is our Alpha and Omega, our beginning and our end.

Sometimes it is hard for us to be still. We are still in the flesh, but nevertheless, He said, "be still." He will not leave us nor forsake us. He is standing in the gap for us.

Sometimes we don't know what to say or pray for. If we could just say, "Jesus, let your will be done," then He will take our cares on to the Father. He is sitting at His right hand pleading our case to God. Remember, the Word said, "God is... a very present help in trouble." He has not forgotten about us at all.

When Moses was leading the people out of Egypt, God gave Moses commandments to give to the people, so Moses asked God the question, "what shall I say unto them?"

He said tell them "I AM THAT I AM." (EXODUS 3:13-14)

So, no matter what we go through, He said I AM, meaning, your bread, water, job, house, mother, father, problem solver... whatever; it all comes under the heading of: I AM.

When we have exhausted all of our resources, I AM is a present help in time of need. That is a promise that we can stand on.

In this chaotic world we live in, it is truly a blessing to know He is here for us. We can have security when all else is insecure, just by knowing that He is a present help. That is another promise that we can stand on to get us through each and every tragedy that we will face.

When we know the Word of God, we can remind ourselves of what he promised us in His Word, then peace and comfort will come upon us.

David said in Psalms 63:7: "...thou hast been my help, therefore in the shadow of thy wings will I rejoice." Then he reminds us in Psalms 145:4 that each generation should always "...praise thy works to another, and shall declare thy mighty acts." Not only should we look to God for our refuge, but we should teach those around us about the good He has done in our lives.

I have been down and He lifted me, time and time again. There is no limit to what God can and will do, and I live my life as a witness to testify this truth to those around me.

His Love is so fulfilling that "...he hath chosen us in Him before the foundation of the world..." (Ephesian 1:4) So before the actual Earth was formed, He loved the idea, the essence, of us and desired us to draw to Him to protect us.

Jesus said in Matthew 11:28-30:

"Come unto me, all ye that labour and are heavy laden, and I will give you rest.

Take my yoke upon you, and learn of me; for I am meek and lowly in heart: and ye shall find rest unto your souls.

For my yoke is easy, and my burden is light."

Those are just more of His promises that we can stand on. We can give Him all of our troubles and He will see us through them all. So from the very small minute that things come before us, we can give them all to Him. Why? Because He is a Present help in time of need.

During times of stress, tribulation, and trepidation, I like to visit these scriptures to remind myself of those promises of God being a shelter, a comforter, and a shield for myself and my life:

Psalms 91:1-2:

"He that dwelleth in the secret place of the most High shall abide under the shadow of the Almighty. I will say of the LORD, He is my refuge and my fortress: my God; in him will I trust."

Psalms 46:10-11:

"Be still, and know that I am God: I will be exalted among the heathen, I will be exalted in the earth.

The Lord of hosts is with us; the God of Jacob is our refuge."

Now we can say, "He is my Refuge and my Fortress: my God; in Him will I trust." Why?

Because He is our Refuge and Our Strength.

Questions

What is an area in your life where God offers you a lot of refuge?

_____
_____
_____
_____

What scripture do you remind yourself of when you're going through a tough period?

_____
_____
_____
_____

Was there a moment when you needed God to show up and He did? What happened?

_____
_____
_____
_____

What is a comfort that you need daily?

_____
_____
_____
_____

Day 17

"He is my Calm Within the Storm"

Psalms 34:17-19"

The righteous cry, and the LORD heareth, and delivereth them out of all their troubles. The LORD is nigh unto them that are of a broken heart; and saveth such as be of a contrite spirit. Many are the afflictions of the righteous: but the LORD delivereth him out of them all."

We all, at some time or another, will or have been through some storms, difficulties, and challenges in life. One of the enemy's traps is to try and isolate us and then convince us that we will not make it.

Let's look at what the Bible says:

1 John 5:14-15:

"And this is the confidence that we have in Him, that, if we ask any thing according to His Will, He heareth us: And if we know that He hear us, whatsoever we ask, we know that we have the petitions that we desired of Him."

Deuteronomy 4:31:

"(For the Lord thy God is a merciful God;) He will not forsake thee, neither destroy thee, nor forget the covenant of thy fathers which He sware unto them."

As we look at those two scriptures, we know that there is calm within the storm, and it comes from the promises He made; and they still hold true today. God promised to deliver the righteous out of all of our afflictions. Standing on God's promises, we can tell Satan, "you have no victory here".

We know that though many are the afflictions of the righteous,

He will delivery us out of them all. He calls us righteous because of our relationship with His Son, Jesus Christ. We are righteous simply by having faith in Him and believing and standing on His Word.

Look at these scriptures as evidence:

Genesis 18:14

"Is anything too hard for the LORD?

Our answer should be NO!

Jeremiah 32:17

"...There is nothing too hard for thee."

If we keep an attitude of faith and expectancy, we will have the calm within the midst of the storm. And whatever we are expecting Him to do in our lives, we can call it done by faith in our Lord and Savior.

So, no matter what we are going through, or are about to go through, the joy of the Lord is our strength and we can be assured that victory is on the way because God is faithful to everything He said in His Word. He made a covenant with our forefathers and we are heirs to all of them.

Sometimes God will say not yet, but with faith and patience we will inherit the promises that He has made in His Word, but they will come in His time.

There may be moments when our ability to trust Him is severely tested. But He has the ability to do just what He said He would do. There is nothing too hard for God. Even when the situation may seem to be getting worse every day, we must still hold on to our faith.

Matthew 17:20 tells us about mustard seed faith. A mustard seed is a very small seed, and that is all that is necessary. Just a little faith in God will get us through the miraculous things that we are facing, or about to face. We can speak to any situation and it will be removed.

But what about those times when we do falter? Well, we can be redeemed through our Father.

Psalms 34:22

"The Lord redeemeth the soul of His servants: and none of them that trust in Him shall be desolate."

That is another promise of God for His people. Even though most storms last longer than we prefer them to, all we need to do is keep in mind that Jesus is in the midst of the storm with us. There is peace within the storm.

He promised us joy and peace. He is leading us to a place where there will be peace and contentment. He has promised us that He will be there with us and for us. All we have to do is keep the faith.

When He brings us out of our situations, we will be free of fear, and be able to trust Him even more, no matter what. He said in Romans 8:28: "...all things work together for good to them that love God..." We might not always see the good, but He said it, and it will come to pass, because He is in the midst of the situation with us. He promised never to leave us nor forsake us.

As David has prophesied to us in Psalms 23:3: "He restoreth my soul: He leadeth me in the paths of righteousness for His name's sake." If He restored David's soul, He can, and will, do the same for us.

His Word does not change.

Questions

What was a recent storm that you were in where you felt God's presence?

_____
_____
_____
_____

In what ways do you feel God calming you in times of trouble?

_____
_____
_____
_____

Has there ever been a moment when you felt like something was too hard for God?

_____
_____
_____
_____

How did God prove you wrong that nothing was too hard for Him?

_____
_____
_____
_____

What is a current struggle that you are waiting for God to deliver you from?

_____
_____
_____
_____

How will you keep yourself encouraged while God works in your favor?

_____
_____
_____
_____
_____

Day 18

"I Will be Fearless"

2 Timothy 1:7

"For God hath not given us the spirit of fear; but of power, and of love, and of a sound mind."

Though the enemy works against us, sometimes our biggest enemy is our own mind. There are times that God has placed a calling, a desire, or an urging in our hearts and in our lives. However, when we start to work toward what God wants, our fear might get the better of us and cause us to hesitate, or even avoid the act. This disobedience can be detrimental to our growth in Christ, and the growth that others are depending on us.

There are many examples in the Bible of people who worked past their fear of potential circumstances to continue to worship God. One of the most recognizable stories is that of Shadrach, Meshach and Abed-nego.

During the rule of King Nebuchadnezzar, he made an edict that His image was the only one to be worshiped, and for those who didn't worship him, they would meet a fiery death.

This plan was a trap to set up these three young men, and the bait was fear. Nebuchadnezzar was trying to place fear in their hearts as a way of submitting to his will. However, Shadrach, Meshach and Abed-nego feared God more.

When we speak of fearing God, it is in a different sense than the fear that Nebuchadnezzar was trying to instill in the people of Babylon.

The "fear" that we should have of God is one of respect and reverence, the same that children have for their parents, adults have for their bosses, and that the nation has for political officials. In Isaiah 35:4, we're told: "Say to them *that are* of a fearful heart, Be strong, fear not: behold, your God will come *with* vengeance, *even* God *with* a recompence; he will come and save you."

God has no intentions of intimidating us, but of loving us, and protecting us.

Nebuchadnezzar had no such noble intentions, and sought to make an example of Shadrach, Meshach and Abednego to guarantee fear in those who loved God into worshiping him.

However, in Daniel 3:16-18, after the three men were captured for breaking the king's law, they were fearless:

"Shadrach, Meshach, and Abed-nego, answered and said to the king, O Nebuchadnezzar, we are not careful to answer thee in this matter. If it be so, our God whom we serve is able to deliver us from the burning fiery furnace, and he will deliver us out of thine hand, O king. But if not, be it known unto thee, O king, that we will not serve thy gods, nor worship the golden image which thou hast set up."

Now imagine if they were afraid? Imagine if they pretended to worship the king just to save themselves. What if they allowed fear to dictate how they behaved, then we wouldn't have such a strong testimony from their story.

The story continues in verses 23 to 25:

"And these three men, Shadrach, Meshach, and Abed-nego, fell down bound into the midst of the burning fiery furnace. Then Nebuchadnezzar the king was astonished, and rose up in haste, and spake, and said unto his counsellors, Did not we cast three men bound into the midst of the fire? They answered and said unto the king, True, O king. He answered and said, Lo, I see four men loose, walking in the midst of the fire, and they have no hurt; and the form of the fourth is like the Son of God."

Their faith was so strong that God even allowed their enemy to be a living witness to His faithfulness to those who act despite of their fear. Though we might be afraid of the circumstances of the world, we must always remember that God is standing in the midst with us.

Then, our actions of faith will become a powerful testimony for all to witness.

Questions

When was there a time that you allowed fear to stop you?

_____
_____
_____
_____

When was there a time that you ignored your fear and acted out on faith?

_____
_____
_____
_____

How has God rewarded your faithfulness in the past?

_____
_____
_____
_____

When was a time that you personally felt God in the midst of trouble, protecting you?

_____
_____
_____
_____

Day 19

"I Relinquish my Burdens to God"

Psalms 55:22

"Cast thy burden upon the LORD, and he shall sustain thee: he shall never suffer the righteous to be moved."

Imagine that you must carry a 50 pound weight on your back every single day. For some people, the initial pressure of the weight might not be a problem, even carrying it for a while could be an easy task. However, the more you carry that weight, the more it begins to tire you. It will wear your body down. It will cause unneeded tension and stress on your body and give you pain.

After a while, you'll want to put that weight down, and might do whatever you could to lessen your unnecessary load.

That is what a burden is; it's an unnecessary load. However, no matter how unnecessary it is, humans can have a horrible habit of picking it up when we don't have to.

The weight of a burden can be tasking, and if you add multiple burdens, it can cause us to experience mental and spiritual fatigue. That's why we have a God that encourages us to put our burdens down.

God's strength is exponentially stronger than ours, and never tiring. So when God sees us struggling, His desire for us is to lighten our load, and carry whatever is weighing us down.

Jesus tells us in Matthew 11:28-30:

"Come unto me, all ye that labour and are heavy laden, and I will give you rest.

Take my yoke upon you, and learn of me; for I am meek and lowly in heart: and ye shall find rest unto your souls.

For my yoke is easy, and my burden is light."

Jesus knows our strength, and He knows His own. He knew that He would be strong enough to carry the burdens of the world, but due to His love for us, He was prepared for it. Because of this, He begs us to exchange our burdens with Him.

What is Jesus' burden? It's everlasting life, love, and peace in the storms of this world.

Jesus is offering this lightened load for our heavy ones from our everyday lives and sins. It is up to us if we continue to carry it or give it to God. Just like the imaginary weight from the beginning of this chapter, if you had the chance to put down a weight that was causing you pain, wouldn't you gladly put it down? Wouldn't you want to relinquish the unnecessary pain and pressure that was put on you?

That is the same thing that God wants for us. He sees our pain, and knows that we don't have to dwell in it. God gave us Jesus to allow us to exchange that pain for peace, love, and happiness. So why would you continue to carry something negative if you didn't have to?

Drop it. Let it go, and grab the freedom that God has made readily available to you.

Questions

What burdens do you find yourself still carrying?

_____
_____
_____
_____

Why do you think you keep holding on to them?

_____
_____
_____
_____

What can you do when you find yourself wanting to pick up an old burden?

_____
_____
_____
_____

Day 20

"I will not dwell in the Past"

Isaiah 43:18-19

"Remember ye not the former things, neither consider the things of old. Behold, I will do a new thing; now it shall spring forth; shall ye not know it? I will even make a way in the wilderness, and rivers in the desert."

What do our eyes, our head, our feet, and a driver's seat all have in common? They all face forward. These things are designed for us to move forward. We are designed for onward progression, and if any of those above named things were facing in the opposite direction, we would no longer be moving forward.

With all that in mind, there is a problem that can sometimes arise in life -the desire to dwell in the past.

As God grew weary of the sin that consumed the cities of Sodom and Gomorrah, He was touched by the pure nature of Lot's heart. By identifying Lot as a righteous man, God sent angels to appear to him in order to warn him of the destruction that He had planned for the two cities.

Genesis 19:15:

"And when the morning arose, then the angels hastened Lot, saying, Arise, take thy wife, and thy two daughters, which are here; lest thou be consumed in the iniquity of the city."

There was only one stipulation God had for a successful exit: do not look back.

God knows that there are very few things that can be gained by dwelling in the past. In fact, most times it hinders our forward progress.

Don't be confused with the notion of not learning from the past. For Romans 15:4 tells us: "For whatsoever things were written aforetime were written for our learning, that we through patience and comfort of the scriptures might have hope." The Bible, and our past experiences, are examples for us to take nuggets of knowledge from in order to continue on the path that God has for our lives. But when we constantly relive negative moments from our past, and are beating ourselves up due to it, we're no longer in a receptive stage of learning. We're in a static state of torment. We're not moving; we're just staying in the same place that we were in during that time of disappointment and sin.

God doesn't desire for His people to be stressed with the sins of the past, but to focus on the redemption of the future. In order for us to reach that redemption, we must stop looking in the past and work to go forward.

In the example of Lot and his family's escape from Sodom and Gomorrah, we see that there was a penalty for looking back, and Lot's wife experienced it.

Genesis 19: 24-26:

"Then the LORD rained upon Sodom and upon Gomorrah brimstone and fire from the LORD out of heaven;

And he overthrew those cities, and all the plain, and all the inhabitants of the cities, and that which grew upon the ground.

But his wife looked back from behind him, and she became a pillar of salt."

Lot's wife became a monument, a testament of the importance of keeping your eyes forward and leaving negativity in the past. That is surely a lesson that we can learn from her past mistake, and one that we must work hard not to perpetuate.

Questions

What keeps you dwelling in the past?

_____
_____
_____
_____

What ways have you attempted to let your past go?

_____
_____
_____
_____

What are some of the positive lessons you have picked up from your past?

_____
_____
_____
_____

What are some of the negative lessons you need to leave behind?

_____
_____
_____
_____

Day 21

"I will Speak Positivity into my Life"

Proverbs 18:21

"Death and life *are* in the power of the tongue: and they that love it shall eat the fruit thereof."

In Genesis 1:27, we read: "So God created man in His own image, in the image of God created He him; male and female created He them." Due to that, we share abilities that God has. So when we see the power that God has over words, we have to know that we have that same power.

To create the world, God simply spoke it into existence. Genesis 1:3-16:

"And God said, Let there be light: and there was light.

And God saw the light, that it was good: and God divided the light from the darkness.

And God called the light Day, and the darkness he called Night. And the evening and the morning were the first day.

And God said, Let there be a firmament in the midst of the waters, and let it divide the waters from the waters.

And God made the firmament, and divided the waters which were under the firmament from the waters which were above the firmament: and it was so.

And God called the firmament Heaven. And the evening and the morning were the second day.

And God said, Let the waters under the heaven be gathered together unto one place, and let the dry land appear: and it was so.

And God called the dry land Earth; and the gathering together of the waters called he Seas: and God saw that it was good.

And God said, Let the earth bring forth grass, the herb yielding seed, and the fruit tree yielding fruit after his kind, whose seed is in itself, upon the earth: and it was so.

And the earth brought forth grass, and herb yielding seed after his kind, and the tree yielding fruit, whose seed was in itself, after his kind: and God saw that it was good.

And the evening and the morning were the third day.

And God said, Let there be lights in the firmament of the heaven to divide the day from the night; and let them be for signs, and for seasons, and for days, and years:

And let them be for lights in the firmament of the heaven to give light upon the earth: and it was so.

And God made two great lights; the greater light to rule the day, and the lesser light to rule the night: he made the stars also."

In that series of scriptures, we see example, after example, after example of God just simply speaking things into existence; from the land that we walk, the air we breathe, to the vegetation that grows from the ground. All these things exist due to a flicker of God's tongue. Is there no wonder that God warns us to be careful of the words that we speak over our lives?

In Psalms 34:12-13, David explains to us: "What man is he that desireth life, and loveth many days, that he may see good? Keep thy tongue from evil, and thy lips from speaking guile."

The words that we speak have a direct correlation to our projection in life. Just like the common phrase that lets us know "our attitude determines our altitude;" our words are the foundation to our attitudes, way of thinking, behaving, and believing.

Words have more power than we could ever imagine. The Bible compares this small, but mighty, appendage to the helm of a ship.

James 3:4-6:

"Behold also the ships, which though they be so great, and are driven of fierce winds, yet are they turned about with a very small helm, whithersoever the governor listeth.

Even so the tongue is a little member, and boasteth great things. Behold, how great a matter a little fire kindleth!

And the tongue is fire, a world of iniquity: so is the tongue among our members, that it defileth the whole body, and setteth on fire the course of nature; and it is set on fire of hell."

Because of these things, it is essential for us to speak positivity into our lives. Not only should we keep our minds on good things, but speak those things as well. If not, we can derail the blessings that God has for us, just by speaking the wrong words.

If God has the ability to create the heavens and the earth with words, remember that you have that same ability to create success or failure in all of your situations.

Questions

Do you find that you're more positive or negative in your speech?

_____
_____
_____
_____

In what ways can you become more positive?

_____
_____
_____
_____

Has there been a situation that you spoke into existence?

_____
_____
_____
_____

What ways can you train your mind to speak more positively?

_____
_____
_____
_____

Day 22

"I will Tune into God, while Tuning out Others"

Proverbs 12:17-23

"He that speaketh truth sheweth forth righteousness: but a false witness deceit. There is that speaketh like the piercings of a sword: but the tongue of the wise is health. The lip of truth shall be established for ever: but a lying tongue is but for a moment. Deceit is in the heart of them that imagine evil: but to the counsellors of peace is joy. There shall no evil happen to the just: but the wicked shall be filled with mischief. Lying lips are abomination to the LORD: but they that deal truly are his delight. A prudent man concealeth knowledge: but the heart of fools proclaimeth foolishness."

The same way we have to be careful with the words that come from our mouths, we must also be careful about the words that come from others.

We are fully aware that we can't control what people say, but we can control who we share our space with. There are some people who have proved to be detrimental to our lives by the negative words that they speak.

Like the old adage, "misery loves company," negative people will speak not only negativity in their own lives, but in others' as well. Those are people who should be kept at bay.

Though God calls us to preach to the masses without prejudice, He also warns us to not get too close to people who cannot control their tongues.

In the book of Job, we meet the titular man who was blessed by God. He was used as an example of unfailing faith. God allowed the devil to test Job by destroying the laugh Job knew and held dear. After Job was left penniless, lost dear family members, and was covered in sores and boils, the only remnant of his former, glorious life was his wife.

This woman stayed with him through all his moments of spiritual winter, and Job could have easily have kept her counsel in his life. But when she began to tell him to stop being faithful to God, that was when Job distanced himself from her. In Job 2:9-10, she approaches Job and speaks negativity into his already dire situation: "Then said his wife unto him, Dost thou still retain thine integrity? curse God, and die. But he said unto her, Thou speakest as one of the foolish women speaketh. What? shall we receive good at the hand of God, and shall we not receive evil? In all this did not Job sin with his lips."

Neither Job, nor his wife, knew that his blessings hinged on if he cursed God, or stayed faithful to Him. But the truth was, if Job would have verbally turned on God, then Satan would have won, and Job would have stayed destitute.

The story of Job is one of mystery because: If Job was seen as good in God's eyes, why would God allow him to suffer? Maybe the answer lies in the fact that Job's faithfulness served as an example to us as proof that not only does being faithful pay off, but ignoring the counsel of those who don't mean us well is integral to our blessings.

Sometimes these people don't mean anything by saying negative things. Like us, everyone must learn to speak positivity into their own lives. We must allow people grace as they try to find the right path that God has for their lives.

However, we must not allow them and their words to hinder us and our potential for growth and blessings.

Questions

Are there people currently in your life who try to speak negativity into your life?

_____
_____
_____
_____
_____

Would it be better to teach them how to speak positively, or to distance yourself from them?

_____
_____
_____
_____
_____

How can others' words affect our future?

_____
_____
_____
_____
_____

Day 23

"I am a Bumblebee"

Mark 10:27

"And Jesus looking upon them saith, With men it is impossible, but not with God: for with God all things are possible."

The analogy of a bumblebee might seem odd, but I believe that all Christians should strive to be like the bumblebee.

If you look at the anatomy of the bumblebee, it has a large, round body with small wings. According to the laws of aerodynamics, this insect should be incapable of flying. However, the summer is lousy with bumblebees flying around, ruining picnics, and scaring people.

But how can that be if the laws of aerodynamics is supposed to assign this insect to be bound to the ground? It is because the bumblebee doesn't know that it's not supposed to fly.

The bumblebee has the instinct to fly, and does so without hesitation and fear. That's the way God calls us to be.

We are not supposed to think about what's impossible because we serve a God that doesn't allow us to be bound by the theories of the world. When the world tells us to sin, God tells us to rise above. Even though it might seem as though rising above is impossible, we know that everything that God has for us is in the realm of possibility.

In Matthew 6:26-33 Jesus addresses the disciples and their lack of faith in how God will provide for them:

"Behold the fowls of the air: for they sow not, neither do they reap, nor gather into barns; yet your heavenly Father feedeth them. Are ye not much better than they?

Which of you by taking thought can add one cubit unto his stature?

And why take ye thought for raiment? Consider the lilies of the field, how they grow; they toil not, neither do they spin:

And yet I say unto you, That even Solomon in all his glory was not arrayed like one of these.

Wherefore, if God so clothe the grass of the field, which to day is, and to morrow is cast into the oven, shall he not much more clothe you, O ye of little faith?

Therefore take no thought, saying, What shall we eat? or, What shall we drink? or, Wherewithal shall we be clothed?

(For after all these things do the Gentiles seek:) for your heavenly Father knoweth that ye have need of all these things.

But seek ye first the kingdom of God, and his righteousness; and all these things shall be added unto you."

Jesus is trying to illustrate to the disciples that they should preach without worry about of how they will be supported because God already has that under control.

The same way the bumblebee doesn't worry about how it will fly, we should be in the same way when it comes to ministry and our own abilities.

Questions

What causes you to question your own abilities?

_____
_____
_____
_____

Is there something that you want to accomplish but worry that you won't be able to achieve?

_____
_____
_____
_____

What ways do you try to strengthen your faith?

_____
_____
_____
_____

Day 24

"I Will Walk in Charity/Love"

I Corinthians 13:1-3

"Though I speak with the tongues of men and of angels, and have not charity, I am become as sounding brass, or a tinkling cymbal. And though I have the gift of prophecy, and understand all mysteries, and all knowledge; and though I have all faith, so that I could remove mountains, and have not charity, I am nothing. And though I bestow all my goods to feed the poor, and though I give my body to be burned, and have not charity, it profiteth me nothing."

While Paul was preaching to the people of Corinth, he touches on the importance of charity. Charity is synonymous with love, but not the love in an intimate relationship, but Agape love; Christ's love. This love is unconditional and extends to everyone, and Paul explains that no matter how phenomenal his abilities in Christ are, if he doesn't have love in his heart, it is all meaningless.

God operates in love. It was His Love that created us. His love that sustains us. His Love that guides us, and His Love that made him sacrifice Jesus just for us. Jesus tells us in John 3:16: "For God so loved the world, that He gave His only begotten Son, that whosoever believeth in Him should not perish, but have everlasting life."

As His children, we must follow in the footsteps of our Father and operate in the same love that He has for us. We must adapt a Love that is not conditional and contingent on if people behave in the way that we want them to, because if that was the case with us, God never would have given us Jesus as a means for salvation. As humans, we have sin by nature, and our behavior can be very self-serving. However, God's Love is designed to cradle us, despite our wrongs, and offer a sense of calm in moments of storm. God's Love doesn't end, and that's the way we should strive to be.

I Corinthians 13:4-8a:

"Charity suffereth long, and is kind; charity envieth not; charity vaunteth not itself, is not puffed up,

Doth not behave itself unseemly, seeketh not her own, is not easily provoked, thinketh no evil;

Rejoiceth not in iniquity, but rejoiceth in the truth;

Beareth all things, believeth all things, hopeth all things, endureth all things.

Charity never faileth:"

As Paul breaks down everything that love is and isn't, we're given a guide in how we should behave in a way that is pleasing to our Father.

Since we are human, we are going to struggle with these things. We're going to have moments of envy, be easily angered, and sin. God knows this about us, but loves us regardless.

A good way to determine if we are loving in the way that God is, is to take the verses in I Corinthians 13:4-7 and replace the word "charity/love" with our names, then ask ourselves is it true. "Am I long suffering? Do I envy? Do I exalt myself, and am puffed up? Do I seek my own? Am I easily provoked? Do I think of evil? Do I rejoice in iniquity? Do I rejoice in the truth?"

Once you place yourself in those verses, you can then begin to see what you need to work on, and how you can build your love in the way that God has built His.

Questions

Based on the scriptures in I Corinthians 13, what part of your love do you need to work on?

_____
_____
_____
_____
_____

Do you remember a specific time when God loved you while you were at your worst?

_____
_____
_____
_____
_____

What might hinder you to love others unconditionally?

_____
_____
_____
_____
_____

Day 25

"I will Forgive Like I want to be Forgiven"

Matthew 6:14-15

"For if ye forgive men their trespasses, your heavenly Father will also forgive you: But if ye forgive not men their trespasses, neither will your Father forgive your trespasses."

As Jesus taught the disciples how to pray, He mentioned the notion of forgiving others. Jesus let the disciples know that this is the way that we should always come to God, our Father, and after confessing our sins to God, we are tasked by Jesus to forgive those who have sinned against us.

The importance of this shows just how flawed we are as humans, and how no one is better than anyone else.

When someone has wronged us, it is very easy to feel exalted and look down on them. It is natural to want to keep score and relive the pain that this person put on us. However, what is that profiting us? What do we gain by staying in a state of pain by remembering the hurtful things someone has done to us? We gain nothing.

God wants His people to progress and to be successful, but we can't if we hold unforgiveness in our hearts. Just like the burdens that God tells us that He will take for us, we have the option to either give it all to God, or continue to let it wear us down.

But if you look closely at the prayer, there's a clue that will help you to forgive others, if you're struggling with letting hurt go. Before you ask God to forgive those who have hurt you, God wants you to confess your sins first.

This act of confession is meant to humble us and remind us that we are not perfect. As we realize how readily God is to forgive us for the sins we commit, we can see just how easily someone else can sin against us.

There is a notion that people tend to judge others by their actions, but themselves by their intentions. By admitting how wrong you are toward God, the one Being in our lives that has only wanted to help us, it's easy to see how someone else can get beside themselves and hurt us.

Sometimes their actions are intentional. Other times the actions are not. But regardless of whether they mean to inflict pain on us is irrelevant, we are called to forgive them - no matter what the offense is.

As we know, God is Love, and through that love is ever-growing forgiveness.

If we strive to be like God, we must also walk in love and forgive, that way we can too be forgiven.

Questions

What usually stops you from forgiving others?

_____
_____
_____
_____
_____

Is there any unforgiveness that you're holding in your heart right now?

_____
_____
_____
_____
_____

How are you able to gain closure after forgiving someone for a past offense?

_____
_____
_____
_____
_____

What sins do you find that God constantly forgives you for?

_____
_____
_____
_____
_____

Day 26

"I will Give Myself the Benefit of the Doubt"

Jeremiah 31:3

"The LORD hath appeared of old unto me, *saying*, Yea, I have loved thee with an everlasting love: therefore with lovingkindness have I drawn thee."

Imagine someone who you love dearly that you would protect from anything. This person can be your best friend, your child, your sibling, spouse, or anyone who you care for deeply. Now, if someone was being abusive to them, wouldn't you try to intervene in some way? Would you stand by idly while someone berated them and told them that they were no good?

Chances are, you would tell them to ignore the words of that horrible person, and you would remind them of their worth.

This course of action should be taken when the victim of condescension is you, and also, when the perpetrator is you as well.

Sometimes we can be so hard on ourselves. We'll use debilitating language when thinking of ourselves and our mistakes; language that we would be appalled if someone said it to our loved ones. However, we'll find no problem being mean to ourselves.

Ephesians 5:29-30:

"For no man ever yet hated his own flesh; but nourisheth and cherisheth it, even as the Lord the church:

For we are members of his body, of his flesh, and of his bones."

The Lord sees us as the precious vessels that we are, and He treats us with patience, love and forgiveness. When we bash ourselves, it is as though we are bashing God and telling Him that He is wrong for loving us. We know that God doesn't make mistakes.

In John 15:9-15, Jesus lays out the case of importance to God and to Him:

"As the Father hath loved me, so have I loved you: continue ye in my love. If ye keep my commandments, ye shall abide in my love; even as I have kept my Father's commandments, and abide in his love. These things have I spoken unto you, that my joy might remain in you, and that your joy might be full. This is my commandment, That ye love one another, as I have loved you. Greater love hath no man than this, that a man lay down his life for his friends. Ye are my friends, if ye do whatsoever I command you. Henceforth I call you not servants; for the servant knoweth not what his lord doeth: but I have called you friends; for all things that I have heard of my Father I have made known unto you."

If Jesus is proud to call us His friends, who are we to abuse that friendship by being mean to ourselves? We are commanded to love one another, and that means that we need to love ourselves. Without true love, like Paul explained to the people of Corinth, are labors for the Lord are in vain.

Therefore, we should love one another, but most importantly, love ourselves by allowing some grace.

Questions

Is there something that you're struggling to forgive yourself for?

_____
_____
_____
_____

Do you find that it's easier or harder to forgive yourself or other people?

_____
_____
_____
_____

What are some of your strongest attributes?

_____
_____
_____
_____

What makes you a great friend?

_____
_____
_____
_____

Day 27

"I will gladly take God with Me Everywhere I go"

Joshua 1:9

"Have not I commanded thee? Be strong and of a good courage; be not afraid, neither be thou dismayed: for the LORD thy God *is* with thee whithersoever thou goest."

There are certain things in our lives that are meant to travel with us. As an adult, you know the importance of bringing your ID, money, and the keys to your domicile. Without those things, you are severely limited in how far you can go, or what you can do. This is the same with your Christian walk if you try to leave God at home.

Your relationship with God shouldn't be relegated only to your time in church, when you read your Bible, or when you listen to Christian music. God is more than a parable that you remember from Bible study, and a lyric from a song.

Compartmentalizing God for only suitable moments is more of a hindrance than you know.

God is our Father, our Creator, our Beginning and our End. With that knowledge, we should proudly bring Him with us every place we go.

With each step that we take, we can either walk in light or darkness. But when we're in darkness, God is our light, our beacon to the safe places of our souls. If you leave God at home, in church, or just around your Bible, it is as if you're leaving without your shoes, your keys, your navigation, your ID, and your car.

Yes, you'll still be able to move, but your actions are limited. You wouldn't be able to move as fast as you'd like, or venture into certain businesses, or reveal your true identity to people. God is all of those things and more.

In John 16:33, Jesus tells us: "These things I have spoken unto you, that in Me you will have peace. In the World you will have tribulation: but be of good cheer; I have overcome the world."

Jesus lets us know that we're going to face hard times, so imagine leaving God home when you really need Him. During rough times and moments of despair, you feel lost and don't know which way to turn. Those are the times that you need God the most, and the times that you should have Him with you.

God is always available to move with us, but we must make a conscious effort to bring Him with us, and do so gladly.

Questions

Describe a time that you left something important to you at home. How did you feel?

_____
_____
_____
_____

How can you remind yourself to take God with you each day?

_____
_____
_____
_____

When do you feel God is closest to you?

_____
_____
_____
_____

When do you feel the most distant from God?

_____
_____
_____
_____

Day 28

"There's Freedom in being Different"

I Peter 2:9

"But ye *are* a chosen generation, a royal priesthood, an holy nation, a peculiar people; that ye should shew forth the praises of him who hath called you out of darkness into his marvellous light:"

In today's world, there is a lot of pressure to conform. There are certain fashion trends that are expected to be adhered to. Social media apps encourage us to share our lives, and there are people who emulate what they see others do. They take similar pictures, use the same filters, and hashtags in an attempt of being part of the status quo.

The status quo isn't bad, but sometimes it can be constricting. In that sense, there's freedom to exist outside of the realm of normality.

In the Bible, we are described as a "peculiar people." In this sense, it doesn't mean that we're bad, it's just that we are different from those who have not accepted Jesus as their savior.

A good illustration of being separate from the people of the world is by examining the life of Daniel.

While Daniel lived in Babylon, he was dedicated to follow God's law, though it contradicted with King Nebuchadnezzar's. One of the first instances was with his diet.

Daniel 1:4-8:

"Children in whom was no blemish, but well favoured, and skilful in all wisdom, and cunning in knowledge, and understanding science, and such as had ability in them to stand in the king's palace, and whom they might teach the learning and the tongue of the

Chaldeans.

And the king appointed them a daily provision of the king's meat, and of the wine which he drank: so nourishing them three years, that at the end thereof they might stand before the king.

Now among these were of the children of Judah, Daniel, Hananiah, Mishael, and Azariah:

Unto whom the prince of the eunuchs gave names: for he gave unto Daniel the name of Belteshazzar; and to Hananiah, of Shadrach; and to Mishael, of Meshach; and to Azariah, of Abednego.

But Daniel purposed in his heart that he would not defile himself with the portion of the king's meat, nor with the wine which he drank: therefore he requested of the prince of the eunuchs that he might not defile himself."

These young men were chosen because they were different from the others. Being different set them apart, and in a way, raised them above others in the kingdom. With these men being seen as so precious, you would imagine that the King would only give them some of the best to eat and drink. King Nebuchadnezzar was working in his best interest to make these men strong.

However, the same intelligence that set Daniel apart, that made the king take note of him, is the same intelligence that forged a bigger gap between him and the other men.

Daniel 1:12-15

"Prove thy servants, I beseech thee, ten days; and let them give us pulse to eat, and water to drink.

Then let our countenances be looked upon before thee, and the countenance of the children that eat of the portion of the king's meat: and as thou seest, deal with thy servants.

So he consented to them in this matter, and proved them ten days.

And at the end of ten days their countenances appeared fairer and fatter in flesh than all the children which did eat the portion of the king's meat."

By forgoing against what the king demanded, Daniel was proved to be more nourished than those who blindly followed the king's eating orders. The men who ate at the king's table, they weren't emaciated. They were filled with plenty of nutrients, and that's how it is in the world. Yes, your needs will be met, but by verging off and following God's life, you will experience exponential nourishment. The things of the natural world are increased in a way that it's now supernatural.

Being different from those around us, being set apart from those in the world, while still living in it, can sometimes seem isolating at times. However, it is in those times that God will bless us.

In Titus 2:13-15, we're told: "Looking for that blessed hope, and the glorious appearing of the great God and our Saviour Jesus Christ; Who gave himself for us, that he might redeem us from all iniquity, and purify unto himself a peculiar people, zealous of good works. These things speak, and exhort, and rebuke with all authority. Let no man despise thee."

Essentially, if God is willing to bless and keep us, who cares what others think of our walk? It is not for us to care or to wonder.

It is for us to follow God, and to do it boldly and unashamed.

Questions

How does your Christian walk set you apart from others?

_____
_____
_____
_____
_____

How has God blessed your walk?

_____
_____
_____
_____
_____

Have you ever felt isolated from others due to your walk?

_____
_____
_____
_____
_____

Is there a way for you to bridge the gap between your walk and ministering to the world?

_____
_____
_____
_____
_____

Day 29

"I will not Waste God's Gifts"

Romans 12:4-8

"For as we have many members in one body, and all members have not the same office: So we, being many, are one body in Christ, and every one members one of another. Having then gifts differing according to the grace that is given to us, whether prophecy, let us prophesy according to the proportion of faith; Or ministry, let us wait on our ministering: or he that teacheth, on teaching; Or he that exhorteth, on exhortation: he that giveth, let him do it with simplicity; he that ruleth, with diligence; he that sheweth mercy, with cheerfulness."

In the same way that our body works in sync with our mind, so does the Body of Christ work with the Word. Though we might not know what, and how, other parts of the Body is moving and acting, we should be focused on using the talents and gifts that God has given us to minister to others.

The Bible lets us know that there are multiple gifts in the Body of Christ, and as a Christian, we need to find what our strengths are. If you're strong in writing, express your love of Christ through a poem, book, song, blog, journal, or note. If your strength lies in alms giving, donate your money, time, or experience to a charity in need.

There are many ways to serve the Kingdom, and with those ways, using your gift is the best way to do so.

So what are some of those gifts? Paul shares it with us in I Corinthians 12:27-30:

"Now ye are the body of Christ, and members in particular.

And God hath set some in the church, first apostles, secondarily prophets, thirdly teachers, after that miracles, then gifts of healings, helps, governments, diversities of tongues.

Are all apostles? are all prophets? are all teachers? are all workers of miracles?

Have all the gifts of healing? do all speak with tongues? do all interpret?"

Once you pinpoint what your Gift of the Spirit is, that is when you will be able to be progressive in the Body of Christ.

Questions

Where do your talents lie?

_____
_____
_____
_____
_____

How have you tried to use your talent to further the Body of Christ?

_____
_____
_____
_____
_____

Are there any other Gifts of the Spirit that suits you and your abilities?

_____
_____
_____
_____
_____

Day 30

"I will Embrace my Destiny"

I Samuel 17:32-37

"And David said to Saul, Let no man's heart fail because of him; thy servant will go and fight with this Philistine. And Saul said to David, Thou art not able to go against this Philistine to fight with him: for thou art but a youth, and he a man of war from his youth. And David said unto Saul, Thy servant kept his father's sheep, and there came a lion, and a bear, and took a lamb out of the flock: And I went out after him, and smote him, and delivered it out of his mouth: and when he arose against me, I caught him by his beard, and smote him, and slew him. Thy servant slew both the lion and the bear: and this uncircumcised Philistine shall be as one of them, seeing he hath defied the armies of the living God. David said moreover, The LORD that delivered me out of the paw of the lion, and out of the paw of the bear, he will deliver me out of the hand of this Philistine. And Saul said unto David, Go, and the LORD be with thee."

David was considered just a child when he made a declaration to kill Goliath. However, it was his destiny to go forth, set a precedence of what faith in God can do, and how He will allow us to have success over the enemy. If David wouldn't have done this, would he have still become king?

Our destinies are written before us, and it is up to us to either go to it fearlessly, or to ignore it.

God has a special calling over our lives and desires for us to embrace the paths that He has set out for us. There will be moments when we see the end game of God's plan for us, but not the dangers that will occur when we try to get to it. Just like David who was destined to be king, he didn't know that his past as a shepherd was going to help him attain the crown.

When David was first placed in the field, charged with watching the sheep, he probably didn't realize just how dangerous it could be. Instead of running from the responsibility, he embraced it. He taught himself how to keep not only himself safe, but the flock as well. Also, when an animal did kidnap one from David's flock, he fearlessly went after the animal to retrieve it.

With this bravery, David was able to not only stand up to Goliath, but defeat him. David was embracing his destiny but didn't even know it.

There are certain tasks that are put in our paths that we might want to avoid, but those very same tasks could be the ones that arm us with the abilities to attain the goal God has for our lives.

Fear doesn't work to help, but to derail our mission from furthering the kingdom. Like 2 Timothy 1:7 tells us: "…God hath not given us the spirit of fear, but of power, and of love, and of a sound mind."

Replace the fear and hesitation that you have when approaching the giants that try to stop you from reaching your full potential. Remove the fear and work with power, love and a sound countenance.

These things will help you with achieving your goal, while removing the debris from your chosen path.

Questions

If David never fought Goliath, do you think he still would have become king?

_____
_____
_____
_____

What "giants" are you trying to slay?

_____
_____
_____
_____

How often do you allow fear to stop you from achieving your goals?

_____
_____
_____
_____

How have your experiences in the past helped you in the present?

_____
_____
_____
_____

Day 31

"I will Exercise Agency with Responsibility"

Genesis 3:6

"And when the woman saw that the tree *was* **good for food, and that it** *was* **pleasant to the eyes, and a tree to be desired to make** *one* **wise, she took of the fruit thereof, and did eat, and gave also unto her husband with her; and he did eat."**

We are not mindless robots. God has given us freedom to make our own decisions. God could have easily made us devoid of the power to think freely so He would have no complications with us following me. However, He knew that would not be genuine love.

Genuine love doesn't come by force or manipulation. It comes from allowing a person to freely choose if they want to be in your presence or not.

When God first placed Adam and Eve in the Garden of Eden, He gave them his stipulations: do not eat from the Tree of Knowledge.

God could have sent a legion of angels to guard that tree, He could have placed the tree out of their reach, or not even make it at all. However, He gave Adam and Eve the information to make a decision and allowed them to do so.

In the dialogue of wisdom, God gives us guidance in Proverbs 3:5-7:

"Trust in the LORD with all thine heart; and lean not unto thine own understanding. In all thy ways acknowledge him, and he shall direct thy paths. Be not wise in thine own eyes: fear the LORD, and depart from evil."

God knows the right way to go, and encourages us to heed His direction, but at the end of the day, He won't force us to go neither left nor right.

On this earth, we face multiple decisions every day, and every single one of those options requires us to rely on our past information to form them. With the Word of God, we are given suggestions on which way to turn, but the decisions are ultimately up to us.

Agency is God's gift to us, a gift that He has given out of love. Agency is the ability to make decisions. We have the power to make our own decisions, but it's integral that we are responsible with this power.

Life isn't like a video game, where if you mess up, you have extra lives. We only have one life on this earth and being irresponsible with our decisions can cost us dearly. With each choice that you face, choose wisely and with gratitude.

We do serve a forgiving God. His Spirit dwells inside of us. More clearly, our body is the temple of the Holy Spirit. When we do wrong, just thinking wrong, and even looking wrong or just having a desire of doing something that is not of God, all we have to do is ask for forgiveness and He will do just that.

He created right from wrong when He created the earth. He has given us a choice as to which one to choose.

He is very pleased when we choose right, as opposed to the wrong.

Questions

Is there a decision that you've been wrestling with?

_____
_____
_____
_____

Do you find that your decision-making is similar to what God leads you?

_____
_____
_____
_____

Has there been a decision where you went your own way and not God's?

_____
_____
_____
_____

What did you learn from the results?

_____
_____
_____
_____

Day 32

"Doing what's right might be hard, but it's always worth it"

Genesis 22:10-13

"And Abraham stretched forth his hand, and took the knife to slay his son. And the angel of the LORD called unto him out of heaven, and said, Abraham, Abraham: and he said, Here am I. And he said, Lay not thine hand upon the lad, neither do thou any thing unto him: for now I know that thou fearest God, seeing thou hast not withheld thy son, thine only son from me. And Abraham lifted up his eyes, and looked, and behold behind him a ram caught in a thicket by his horns: and Abraham went and took the ram, and offered him up for a burnt offering in the stead of his son."

Very few of us will face the panic-inducing moment of having to choose between our child and our faith. When Abraham was tasked by God to sacrifice Isaac, his only son, we read how Abraham obediently went along with it until God offered the ram as a sacrifice.

What we don't see is the sweat-induced panic that I'm sure Abraham was in. We don't read about the inner turmoil, tears, and anger that he must have felt to have to lead his son to his own death. But, I'm sure it was there.

Abraham, being an obedient servant to God, followed through with instructions, in hopes that God would deliver him from what he was called to do, and in the end, God did. Abraham's faithfulness was rewarded by a ram.

There are times that God's calling for our lives is going to seem detrimental to the direction that we would like to go down; however, following that path will lead us to God rewarding us.

Sometimes the reward might not seem as great at the moment, but it can have such a wonderful, beautiful payout in the end. How so?

As we follow Jesus's path in the Bible, we see God put Himself in the exact same scenario that He put Abraham in, but we were in Isaac's place. God loved us so much that His sacrificial ram was Jesus.

John 3:16 tells us: "...God so loved the world, that He gave His only begotten Son, that whosoever shall believeth in Him should not perish, but have everlasting life."

In order to save us, God sacrificed His son, so we could have a way to Heaven. God's Word is full of promises of loving us, forgiving us, protecting us, guiding us, and constantly watching out for us. In that painful moment of seeing His Son die a painful death, God did something that was right for us, but painful for Him. Should we not return the favor?

That favor is just giving Him praise and doing what He has commanded us to do. He said He would forgive us and we can stand on His Word.

His Word is true and He is a God that cannot and does not lie.

Questions

What is a painful sacrifice you had to recently make?

_____
_____
_____
_____

Were you able to see the benefits of the sacrifice immediately, or eventually?

_____
_____
_____
_____

How can you strengthen your faith to be able to make sacrifices easier?

_____
_____
_____
_____

What scripture helps to give you comfort during those stressful decision-making times?

_____
_____
_____
_____

Day 33

"I will Seek out True Joy"

Psalms 30:5

"**For his anger** *endureth but* **a moment; in his favour** *is* **life: weeping may endure for a night, but joy** *cometh* **in the morning.**"

In a world of not promised tomorrows, life is too short to focus and dwell in the negative aspects of life. Every single day that we wake up is a gift, and we can either enjoy it, or squander it.

I refuse to believe that our God wants us to be unhappy. God has offered us many options to choose joy over sorrow.

Jesus tells us in John 8:12: "Then spake Jesus again unto them, saying, I am the light of the world: he that followeth me shall not walk in darkness, but shall have the light of life."

Like the previous chapter explains, we have a choice each and every day, and that is to be unhappy, or to actively pursue joy.

In fact, to choose joy is to draw closer to the Lord. Psalms 32:10-11 states: "Many sorrows shall be to the wicked: but he that trusteth in the LORD, mercy shall compass him about. Be glad in the LORD, and rejoice, ye righteous: and shout for joy, all ye that are upright in heart."

Joy allows us to guard our hearts and protect our minds from wickedness. Jesus is the author of our joy, and the source of it.

From the time of Jesus's birth, his presence was followed in joy. When the star led the Wise Men to where He was, there was joy. When Jesus performed miracles, there was joy. Even when explaining His death to His disciples, He tells them in John 16:19-20: "Now Jesus knew that they were desirous to ask him, and said unto them, Do ye enquire among yourselves of that I said, A little while, and ye shall not see me: and again, a little while, and ye shall see me? Verily, verily, I say unto you, That ye shall weep and lament, but the world shall rejoice: and ye shall be sorrowful, but your sorrow shall be turned into joy."

To be near the Father is to be in the realm of joy. All you have to do is grasp it, and bask in the peace and happiness that comes from being close to our Lord and Savior.

No matter what He allows us to go through, He promised us joy and peace.

John 16:33 states "These things I have spoken unto you, that in me ye might have peace. In the world ye shall have tribulation: but be of good cheer; I have overcome the world.

We can stand on His promises.

Questions

How do you find joy when you're feeling down?

_____
_____
_____
_____

How do you seek Christ to increase your joy?

_____
_____
_____
_____

What is your happiest memory?

_____
_____
_____
_____

Did you feel at peace after reliving that memory?

_____
_____
_____
_____

Day 34

"I will Actively Wait"

James 2:14-17

"What doth it profit, my brethren, though a man say he hath faith, and have not works? can faith save him? If a brother or sister be naked, and destitute of daily food, And one of you say unto them, Depart in peace, be ye warmed and filled; notwithstanding ye give them not those things which are needful to the body; what doth it profit? Even so faith, if it hath not works, is dead, being alone."

There might be a misconception that when God has a blessing for us, we should just sit and wait for it to happen. This is false. God calls us to be active, and to perform tasks that will place us in a better situation to readily gain our blessings.

In James 1:22, the Bible explains:

"But be ye doers of the word, and not hearers only, deceiving your own selves."

The scripture lets us know that if we just sit back and wait for God to bless us, then we are deceiving ourselves.

If we expect for God to be active in our lives (interceding, blessing, and calming us), He expects us to do the same (praying, working, and repenting). The gifts that we have should be used as we wait for God's next orders.

As the Body of Christ, we're always moving, growing, and flourishing. We cannot accomplish anything in the Church if we are stagnant.

When we learn of His word, we cannot just sit and wait, we have to put some action behind what He has said.

We are to give Him praise in the midst of our storms and tribulations He allows us to go through.

He is putting a testimony within us, to use us to help others.

Questions

What works do you feel like God is calling you to do?

_____
_____
_____
_____
_____

Do you feel prepared to receive God's blessings? Why?

_____
_____
_____
_____
_____

The Bible calls for us to be doers, but it also calls for us to be still to hear from God. How do you combine the two to be pleasing in God's sight?

_____
_____
_____
_____
_____

Day 35

"I will Quench my Thirst Daily"

Psalms 143:6

"I stretch forth my hands unto thee: my soul *thirsteth* after thee, as a thirsty land. Selah."

In our lives, we can sometimes be in a spiritual desert. Our souls can be parched for a good word, comfort, or just for the knowledge of God. During those times, we should quench our thirst by drawing closer to God, by reading our Bible, following the Word, and spending time with Him.

With our natural bodies, what do we do when we are thirsty? We don't just talk about how our body craves liquid, we seek it. We actively search for some form of nourishment that will help us end our discomfort.

As the natural body can be parallel to the Spiritual Body, it is the same thing. When we begin to feel the discomfort in our spirit due to us not being actively in the Word, we should seek it. We should go after our Father with the same vigor that we do to find a bottle of water/soda/tea or any other beverage that we crave.

Matthew 5:6:

"Blessed are they which do hunger and thirst after righteousness: for they shall be filled."

That is another promise that He made for and to us. All we have to do is call on His name and He hears us and will come and comfort us. He knows what is in our heart and our mind.

Just as a cool beverage promises to quench our thirst, so does the presence of God to our thirsty spirit.

He is our healer time and time again.

Questions

What is your favorite way to quench your spiritual thirst?
_____
_____
_____
_____

How do you feel after you draw nigh to God after a drought?
_____
_____
_____
_____

What ways do you try to stay spiritually hydrated?
_____
_____
_____
_____

Day 36

"Evolve Beyond Traditions"

Colossians 2:8

"Beware lest any man spoil you through philosophy and vain deceit, after the tradition of men, after the rudiments of the world, and not after Christ."

Christianity should strive to be an ever growing journey, not a statue. The difference between the two are truly significant. A statue is stagnant. It doesn't move, it doesn't grow, it is stuck in a perpetual state of existing. However, a journey signifies movement, growth, following a direction and heading to a specific location.

While Jesus was on this earth, He addressed the Pharisees and their traditions. While the Pharisees were Christians by name, they weren't by practice. They neglected the ways of Christ, and the Word, and continued to behave in tradition.

1 Peter 1:18 speaks on how deceptive focusing just on the traditions, but ignoring the Word can be:

"Forasmuch as ye know that ye were not redeemed with corruptible things, *as* silver and gold, from your vain conversation *received* by tradition from your fathers;"

Now, God isn't opposed to traditions, just the ones that people hide behind as an attempt not to actively follow the Word. Let your relationship with God be more than a tradition, let it be an actual relationship that you learn and grow from. God is looking to produce the right seed within us so that we might grow and produce good fruit and a good harvest in order that He might use us for His Glory.

Something to think about:

Who are you spending your time with? Each day He is giving us another chance to get it right.

Our today should be better than our yesterday.

Questions

What is a good example, in the natural world of traditions, removing the true meaning of an activity?

_____
_____
_____
_____
_____

How can traditions hinder growth?

_____
_____
_____
_____
_____

What are the traditions that can help you with your Christian walk?

_____
_____
_____
_____
_____

Day 37

"I will Renew My Mind Daily"
Isaiah 40:28-31

"Hast thou not known? hast thou not heard, that the everlasting God, the LORD, the Creator of the ends of the earth, fainteth not, neither is weary? there is no searching of his understanding. He giveth power to the faint; and to them that have no might he increaseth strength. Even the youths shall faint and be weary, and the young men shall utterly fall: But they that wait upon the LORD shall renew their strength; they shall mount up with wings as eagles; they shall run, and not be weary; and they shall walk, and not faint."

As we age, our body and mind does so as well. With each moment of fatigue, God offers to renew us, to lessen our mental fatigue.

God is like the shower that wakes you up in the morning, or the morning dew that refreshes the grass at dawn.

It's natural to feel mentally tired at times. Stressors can zap us of our energy and our ability to think on good things; so during those times, that's when we must reach out to God, ask Him for renewal, and accept it.

All we have to do is say, "Jesus". And He is there at all times. He promised "…never to leave thee, nor forsake thee."

He is standing on the right side of the Father, looking down, just waiting on us to call His name. He is our help in times of trouble.

His promise is already done; just wait upon Him. And we will be able to walk and not faint.

Asking for help doesn't make us weak, but ignoring that help does.

Questions

When was the last time you felt mentally fatigued?

_____
_____
_____
_____
_____

How did that affect your relationship with Christ?

_____
_____
_____
_____
_____

What means do you use to renew your relationship with God each day?

_____
_____
_____
_____
_____

Day 38

"Tears are not in vain"

John 11:35

"Jesus wept."

Though this scripture is short, it holds great power and shows that Christians can be versatile.

Many scriptures encourage us to find joy, but there are times when we are down. We are going to have moments when we're overwhelmed, depressed, upset, angry, and any other negative emotion.

Being a Christian doesn't negate those feelings. Accepting Jesus as our Savior does not magically make everything immediately better. What becoming a Christian does is give us accessibility to our help.

I believe that we should own our emotions and not hide them. The more you suppress a feeling, the stronger it becomes, and the more likely you are to act out in sin due to not acknowledging how you truly feel.

Psalms 46:1 reminds us that: "God *is* our refuge and strength, a very present help in trouble." Present help is right now, not tomorrow, but right now.

So we can weep if we feel the need to do so.

He promised us that He will rebuild the broken heart and supply all of our needs.

The reason why we have a refuge is because we have emotions. We have weaknesses and trying times, and through those times, we can find joy and guidance. John 16:33 acknowledges our pain by addressing: "These things I have spoken unto you, that in Me ye might have peace. In the world ye shall have tribulation: but be of good cheer; I have overcome the world."

But God is the initial stepping stool to expressing emotions. There are people whose gift from God is to offer counseling, or medical services to those who are in need.

God put it on those people's hearts to work and offer help to those in trouble. If you are one of those who are in trouble, remove any negative stigma from trying to get help. The Lord does not want His people to be in pain, and by praying, spending time in the Word, and utilizing the resources that God has placed on this earth, you will be able to handle anything, eventually.

That is another promise we can stand on.

Tears are not in vain. Why, because Jesus wept.

Questions

Do you express your emotions in a healthy way?
_____
_____
_____
_____

How have others tried to suppress your emotions?
_____
_____
_____
_____

How do you exercise your agency over your emotions?
_____
_____
_____
_____

Do you seek help outside of praying and reading the Bible? If so, what?
_____
_____
_____
_____

Write yourself a letter of appreciation and strength for seeking help below.
_____
_____
_____
_____

Day 39

"I am Worthy"

Psalms 149:4

"For the LORD taketh pleasure in his people: he will beautify the meek with salvation."

In today's world, there is a lot of talk about what's deserved and what's not. We see people on television, magazines, and on the radio, and we might actively judge and say if they should be in the limelight.

Each day, with the help of social media, we broadcast our lives to others, and sometimes their answers to our big news is: "So what?" or "Who cares?". It's very easy to take this same idea to ourselves and our salvation and wonder: "am I really worthy of the things that God has for me?"

The answer is an emphatic "Yes!"

God sees us as treasures that He was willing to sacrifice his one and only Son for, so why should we doubt our blessings? Why should we feel guilty if we are blessed, when that is what God wants to do for us?

God doesn't want us to exalt ourselves over others, but He doesn't want us to lower ourselves either. In the eyes of God, we are all equal, and we are all worthy to be saved.

He is our ALPHA and OMEGA, our beginning and our end. He has control over our lives. He knew us while we were in our mother's womb.

He said we are worthy, so we need to be thankful and give Him the praise for what He has done, and is doing, and is going to do in our lives.

Questions

Do you have moments when you feel unworthy of God's goodness?

_____
_____
_____
_____
_____

Have you ever felt guilty of being blessed?

_____
_____
_____
_____
_____

Have you ever doubted your abilities?

_____
_____
_____
_____
_____

What do you do to find your confidence?

_____
_____
_____
_____
_____

Day 40

The Vine and the Branches

John 15:1-8

"I am the true vine, and my Father is the husbandman. Every branch in me that beareth not fruit he taketh away: and every branch that beareth fruit, he purgeth it, that it may bring forth more fruit. Now ye are clean through the word which I have spoken unto you. Abide in me, and I in you. As the branch cannot bear fruit of itself, except it abide in the vine; no more can ye, except ye abide in me. I am the vine, ye are the branches: He that abideth in me, and I in him, the same bringeth forth much fruit: for without me ye can do nothing. If a man abide not in me, he is cast forth as a branch, and is withered; and men gather them, and cast them into the fire, and they are burned. If ye abide in me, and my words abide in you, ye shall ask what ye will, and it shall be done unto you. Herein is my Father glorified, that ye bear much fruit; so shall ye be my disciples."

In the Old Testament, Israel is referred to as a vine. However, in these verses we find the True Vine is Christ Himself.

The Father is the husbandman, the one that owns the vineyard. And if the branch does not bear good fruit, it is cut off and disposed of.

Since we are branches and we are connected to the Vine and producing fruit, we will be purged and we will bring forth more fruit. He said in Verse 5: "He that abideth in me, and I in him, the same bringeth forth much fruit: for without me ye can do nothing."

If we are not connected to the Vine, we can be pruned and cut off from the Vine. Once the branch is cut off, it withers and dies.

There is a distinct collation between the branch and the Vine.

The life of the branch depends on staying connected to the vine.

To bring it home for us, if we are not connected to the Vine, which is Jesus Christ Himself, we will wither and die spiritually. He is our life source.

Verse 6, tells us that "If a man abide not in me, he is cast forth as a branch, and is withered; and men gather them, and cast them into the fire, and they are burned."

Verse 7, tells us "If ye abide in me, and My Words abide in you, ye shall ask what ye will, and it shall be done unto you."

That promise still holds true for us today. Even though He did not put a time on any of His promises, but if He said it, it will come to pass. And it all hinges on the small word IF.

The Right and Left of our lives rest upon this 2 letter word: IF.

Verse 6 tells us what will happen if we don't,

Verse 7 tells us what will happen if we do.

In order to be a fruitful Christian, we just need to stay connected to the Vine, and allow His Spirit to flow through our lives, and then, and only then, wii we be able to bear much fruit.

How do we stay connected?

Putting Him #1 on our priority list, and having no other God's before Him.

By communicating with Him daily through prayer, praise, and worship.

Studying His Word.

Giving Him the first fruits of the day by being thankful for allowing us to see another day.

Another day gives us another chance to get it right. These are just a few ways of staying connected to the Vine, in order for Him to do His work through us.

When we do our part, and our part is staying connected, He said "we will bring forth much fruit." That is my desire, to bring forth much fruit for Him and not myself. That is one of the requirements for being a disciple.

He said in V 8: "Herein is my Father glorified, that ye bear much fruit; so shall ye be my disciples."

He told His Disciples, "If you keep my commandments, ye shall abide in my love; even as I have kept my Father's commandments, and abide in His love.

Then He said, "These things I have spoken unto you, ...that your joy might be full."

He also told them, "I have chosen you..." "I have called you friends;".

He told them, "These things I command you, that you love one another." Loving others is not a choice, it is a command. V 17.

In order to continue in the joy of the Lord, we have to stay connected to the Vine. All the promises of God will come to pass. His time is not our time, but if He said it, it is already done. We just have to get to that time that He has planned for us.

He maintains all that He says. He created the earth, He put the moon, sun and the stars in place and they are still in place today. That is proof that we can stand on His Word; it is faithful and true.

If He said it, it will be done.

Now we can say, Amen.

Questions

What are the most valuable lessons you have learned from this book?

_____
_____
_____
_____
_____

In what ways do you need to improve your walk with Christ?

_____
_____
_____
_____
_____

In what ways is your praise sufficient?

_____
_____
_____
_____
_____

How do you keep producing more fruit for the Body of Christ?

_____
_____
_____
_____
_____

www.ingramcontent.com/pod-product-compliance
Lightning Source LLC
Chambersburg PA
CBHW051804040426
42446CB00007B/506